ESSEX RAILWAY HERITAGE

The County's Railway Buildings and their History

With an Introduction to Great Eastern Railway Architecture

Peter Kay

CONTENTS

The Halfpenny Pier Ticket Office, Harwich.

LISTED RAILWAY BUILDINGS IN ESSEX
with dates of listing

Audley End station   1971
Audley End tunnel, south portal   1986
Blake Hall station   1984
Braintree station   1989
Brentwood, Seven Arch Bridge   1994
Chappel signal box   1986
Chappel Viaduct   1967
Elsenham up platform waiting rooms   1980
Great Chesterford station   1971
Harlow Town station   1995
Harwich, Great Eastern Hotel   1972
Harwich, Halfpenny Pier booking office and waiting room   1972
Harwich, Train Ferry gantry   1987
Ingatestone station   1976
Littlebury tunnel, south portal   1986
Loughton station   1994
Maldon East station   1969
Mistley station   2005
[Mistley signal box]
Ongar station including coal offices   1984
Roydon station   1971
St Botolph's, C18 station house   1971
Tilbury Riverside station and landing stage   1989
Wivenhoe, goods shed and stables   1988

Also Wickham Bishops viaducts are an 'Ancient Monument'.

INTRODUCTION and ACKNOWLEDGEMENTS

Like so many books, this one began more by accident than design, the byproduct of work originally started solely with the intention of assisting in the preparation of the new edition of Pevsner's *The Buildings of England : Essex* (now due for publication in 2007). It soon became clear that far more material was being acquired than could ever be featured there.

This book, like Pevsner, is concerned principally with buildings and structures which survive today. All buildings and structures mentioned in the text and captions are still standing unless specifically stated to the contrary. Nevertheless, some buildings now gone are referred to as necessary, to put the surviving buildings into proper context and explain the overall development of railway architecture in Essex. (However, no attempt is made to cover the first-generation buildings on the Colchester line and the London Tilbury & Southend line, most of which were replaced at an early date). Many of the buildings now demolished were to the same or similar designs to those that survive.

The subtitle 'With an Introduction to Great Eastern Railway Architecture' is included because there is much more here on the development of GER buildings 1862 – 1922 than has ever appeared in print before. The fact that no substantive analysis of this subject has ever been published, has made it necessary to include a lot more here on the background factors than would otherwise have been necessary. However it must be understood that this book is in no way posing as a complete account (or even a balanced summary) of the subject. Apart from the obvious point that GER architecture could not be covered in full in a book restricted to Essex, it is also the case that study of GER buildings elsewhere has been more in the line of foraying as appropriate than of any comprehensive examination.

In trying to produce a text which is readable both by those with a local heritage or architectural interest but no railway background, and by those with a railway interest but no architectural background, it may be that neither party will feel satisfied!

The book covers *present-day* Essex, including the Thurrock and Southend areas but excluding Havering, Redbridge, Waltham Forest, and Newham (which will be included at a later date in another book covering East London). For coherence of railway geography, though, there are a few exceptions to the rule. Grange Hill, Chigwell and Roding Valley stations will be included in the East London volume along with the other Fairlop Loop stations. Sturmer station is in Essex but cannot sensibly be treated separately from the rest of the Sudbury – Haverhill line, which is in Suffolk. *Per contra*, Bishops Stortford, which is in Hertfordshire, is included here in order to consider a coherent length of the Cambridge line (Roydon to Great Chesterford) in the same place. Great Chesterford station is now in Essex, as the village always was, but at one time it was in Cambridgeshire.

Detailed historical research on many stations had already been carried out by others before this book was conceived, notably by Peter Paye in his books on the Brightlingsea, Tollesbury, Saffron Walden, Thaxted and Bishops Stortford – Braintree branches, and in a good number of articles in the Great Eastern Railway Society's *Great Eastern Journal.* The author's own researches into the many other stations not researched already have succeeded in revealing almost all the most important dates and facts; however it should be understood that, due to the large number of locations involved, this research has not been carried out on the 'no stones unturned' basis that one might now expect in a book restricted purely to one stretch of line.

A fair number of 'period' photographs are included here, but it is impossible to find old views of architectural details, so the majority of such views here were newly taken for the book. All recent photographs not credited or captioned to the contrary were taken by the author in 2001-2006. An appropriate point, perhaps, to note that if British society continues on its present path to anti-photographer paranoia, the production of books such as this will soon become impossible.

It has not been thought necessary to include a map of the Essex railway system, given that the majority of the lines are still open so that any recent map will serve. For investigation of the closed lines (Woodham Ferrers - Maldon, Witham - Maldon, Bishops Stortford - Braintree, Kelvedon - Tollesbury, Chappel - Halstead - Haverhill, Wivenhoe - Brightlingsea, Audley End - Bartlow, and Elsenham - Thaxted), and for locating intermediate structures on other lines, the reader will in any case need the Ordnance Survey Explorer maps. Ordnance Survey grid references ('GR') are given in those cases where the location of a structure might not be obvious otherwise.

As always with a GER-related subject, this book has relied heavily on the many years work carried out at the Public Record Office by Harry Jones, Colin Rose and others in transcribing the GER minute books, and subsequently putting the results on to disk. Another important source now available is the Great Eastern Railway Society's collection of historical records and plans, catalogued by Lyn Brooks and housed at the Essex Record Office.

I am grateful to John Watling for reading through the manuscript. Other assistance was obtained from Gordon Biddle, Peter B.Boyden, Philip J.Cone, Nigel Digby, Graham Kenworthy, Hugh Moffat, Peter Paye, Alic Robertson, Andy Rush, Ian Strugnell and Jerzy Swieszkowski.

The book was put together for the press by Jim Connor to whom again especial thanks are due.

Any corrections received by spring 2007 will be incorporated in a *Corrigenda and Addenda* in the 'Supplement' volume.

Peter Kay
Wivenhoe, June 2006.

Bridge 1057 on the Harwich branch frames the Stour estuary. This original 1854 semicircular-arch underbridge is built in an attractive bright red brick.

3

A second volume

ESSEX RAILWAY
HERITAGE – SUPPLEMENT

is intended to be published in 2007, and will contain a full listing of all surviving railway buildings and structures in Essex, in line order. It will also include much further information on individual stations, including further photographs and plans.

If you are interested in this SUPPLEMENT, or in the further book on

EAST LONDON
RAILWAY HERITAGE

to be published at a future date, please advise the publisher (preferably by email, otherwise by post – addresses on inside front cover) and you will then be informed when publication is imminent. The books will be made available post-free at a special pre-publication price.

Period furniture matches the period glass at Manningtree.

CHAPTER ONE

TWO MAIN LINES: THE EASTERN COUNTIES RAILWAY and the NORTHERN & EASTERN RAILWAY 1836–1845
and subsequent ECR lines to 1862

Railway building in Essex began with the 1836 Acts for the Colchester line (the Eastern Counties Railway) and the Cambridge line (the Northern & Eastern Railway). Both lines were destined to prolonged gestations in the difficult financial climate of the late 1830s and early 1840s. The ECR line was opened to Romford in 1839, Brentwood in 1840, and Colchester in 1843. The N&ER struggled to Bishops Stortford in three stages in 1840-42, and also started on the Bishops Stortford – Newport section before being taken over by the ECR in 1844.

THE COLCHESTER LINE

Nothing remains of the original ECR station buildings of 1839-43 (several of which were only temporary structures) – unless one counts the Ingatestone almshouses which served as the Booking Office for the 1843 temporary station there. In compensation, though, the Shenfield – Colchester section retains a large proportion of its original bridges, partly because it has never been widened. These include two major and several lesser viaducts, the whole of this section of the line being built against the lie of the land, as described by Maj-Gen. Pasley in his March 1843 inspection report:

'The line of this railway intersects the courses of all the little rivers and brooks and crosses the valleys through which they flow. Hence it has a greater number of considerable cuttings and embankments, and has more arches and viaducts....than perhaps any other line of railway of equal extent. This has rendered the works particularly laborious and expensive, and beset with difficulties, which Mr Braithwaite the Engineer in Chief has overcome with great skill and energy'.

Had the ECR continued beyond Colchester as originally intended, there would have been a much more spectacular viaduct over the Stour valley at Flatford.

The ordinary underbridges were mostly of brick, but seven were stated to be of iron. The overbridges were almost all of brick, some single-arch (with three-centred arches) and some three-arch (with segmental arches). Many were of course rebuilt or altered for electrification, but several do remain in original form, not least the well-known Seven Arch Bridge at Brentwood. Yellow London stock bricks were used for most structures to a point east of Chelmsford, and a much more attractive red brick at the Colchester end of the line.

JOHN BRAITHWAITE

John Braithwaite (1797-1870) was trained as a mechanical engineer by his father, the owner of the long-established firm of Braithwaite & Co of London. After the deaths of his father and brother, John ran the company in the 1820s. In 1829 he built the locomotive Novelty *for the Rainhill trials. He became heavily involved with J.C.Robertson the owner of the* Mechanic's Magazine *(then the leading railway paper) and patent agent, and Robertson organised the defence case when Braithwaite was sued for breach of patent over the* Novelty's *boiler. Robertson and Braithwaite were leading figures in the promotion of the ECR in 1834, Robertson becoming Secretary (in which position he instigated the company's slide into financial irregularities), and Braithwaite the 'Acting Engineer' with his friend C.B.Vignoles as 'Consulting Engineer'. After the ECR was subjected to attacks by John Herapath (a former director) in the* Railway Magazine, *Robertson and Briathwaite set up a rival paper of their own, the* Railway Times. *Robertson was dismissed by the ECR Board in 1839 but Braithwaite, despite his reputation for short temper and drunkenness, held on to his job until sacked in May 1843 just after completion of the line to Colchester.*

The old Almshouses in Stock Lane, Ingatestone, date from 1557, and may rank as Britain's oldest 'station building', although their role as such was both limited and short-lived. The Almshouses had been acquired by the ECR for the making of the cutting through the site, and partly demolished. The easternmost of those remaining (at left here) had a door inserted in the end wall and served as Booking Office for the first Ingatestone 'station' which had a fitful existence in 1843/4 until agreement was reached with Lord Petre for a permanent station in Hall Lane. In the meantime Petre had built replacement Almshouses at the other end of town, opened in 1840.

COLCHESTER LINE VIADUCTS	(omits those of one arch only)	
Chelmsford Viaduct (River Can)	GR 702067	18 semicircular arches of 30ft span
Chelmsford Station Viaduct	GR 704070	West of Duke St there are 48 low semicircular arches of 16ft span. The station platforms east of Duke St are also built on viaduct.
Chelmsford (River Chelmer)	GR 714075	3 three-centred arches of 45ft span and 15ft rise
Boreham Mill*	GR 747099	4 three-centred arches of 30ft span and 10ft rise
Hatfield Mill* (River Ter)	GR 781117	3 three-centred arches of 40ft span and 15ft(?) rise
Witham Mill* (River Brain)	GR 818150	4 three-centred arches of 30ft span and 10ft rise
Kelvedon (River Blackwater)	GR 863193	3 three-centred arches of 42ft span and 12ft rise
Lexden (Seven Arch) Viaduct (River Colne)	GR 962261	7 three-centred arches of 50ft span and 16ft 6in rise

*names as given by Pasley

COLCHESTER LINE VIADUCTS AND BRIDGES

top

The largest of the ECR viaducts is the Chelmsford Viaduct over the River Can valley, which forms a conspicuous feature of the town. It is 674ft long with a maximum height of 44ft. Its eighteen six-ring semicircular arches are of 30ft span. It is built in a yellow-brown brick but there has been a lot of patching and, with some bad staining as well, it does not bear too close an inspection ! There is no parapet wall now. This viaduct is on a continuous curve.

second

Most of the arches of the Chelmsford Station Viaduct between Parkway and Duke Street have been boarded in for commercial letting, leaving only the section over Parkway itself in presentable condition. The four-ring semicircular arches are of 16ft span, in yellow brick. The parapet wall remains on this section, with a stone string course at track level. The piers have relieving arches. The viaduct widens towards the station to accommodate the platforms.

third

Duke Street underbridge at Chelmsford (1842) was deemed worthy of special treatment, with stone plinth, quoins and voussoirs, being in yellow brick otherwise. The segmental arch has a rise of only 5ft 6in. This was actually two separate bridges side by side originally, the middle section joining them (which has no stone plinth) being added when the station was converted to a side platform arrangement in 1856.

The Widford Road overbridge at Chelmsford was also deemed worthy of stone voussoirs; this had three segmental arches, of which the outer two remain (the central arch was replaced by a concrete span for electrification).

fourth

The three-arch Chelmer viaduct east of Chelmsford station has seven-ring three-centred arches of 45ft span, and is 34ft high. It retains its parapet wall. All the Colchester line three-centred-arch viaducts had simple stone imposts of this type, and a stone string course at rail level.

Again this viaduct is in yellow brick, with much patching including some in bright red bricks.

bottom left

The River Brain viaduct at Witham, which now also spans Almond Road. Its four five-ring three-centred arches are of 30ft span. The height is only 26ft. As the arches are in red brick, one imagines the whole viaduct was originally, but it has now been refaced to a large extent. The parapet wall has been removed.

below

The Station Road / River Blackwater viaduct at Kelvedon has the flattest arches of any of the Colchester line's three-centred-arch viaducts, 42ft span with 12ft rise. All is in red brick, seemingly largely original. The slope at the top was related to the addition of the footway from the up platform over the viaduct to the Low Level station.

above

Seven Arch Viaduct over the Colne at Lexden must be one of the country's least-known viaducts of significance, however it can be accessed via a footpath. It is in red brick with little patching. The seven seven-ring arches are of 50ft span, and the maximum height is 55ft. The parapet wall has been removed except over the westernmost and easternmost arches. The easternmost pier seems to have experienced difficulties at an early date and is heavily buttressed on its east side in a brick very similar to the original.

first right

Bridge 174 at Blunts Hall Road, Witham (GR 812143) is to an attractive design with pilasters either side of the four-ring semicircular arch, curving wing walls, and stone coping. The span is 14ft 10in. Bridge 204 at Lexden (GR 969263) is very similar. Both are in red brick.

second right

Bridge 176 at Witham (GR 816147) was built as a 23ft span, 38ft long underline 'tunnel' with a five-ring semicircular arch. In such cases the 'tunnel' was built first and the embankment tipped over the top. This bridge is in a pale yellow brick (unlike the other original bridges in Witham). Bridge 198 at Turkey Cock Lane, Stanway (GR 933247) is similarly constructed, in red brick.

bottom right

Of the half-dozen ordinary 1842 Colchester line overbridges remaining in near-original condition, Bridge 191 ('Hanover Bridge') at Feering (GR 876205) is both the most attractive and the most readily seen. The span is 33ft 7in. These bridges have a three-centred arch of five rings with stone imposts, buttressed either side, with end pilasters. There is a two-course curving brick string course above the arch, and the brickwork above this is all in curved courses in parallel. The parapet walls originally had a continuously-curved coping but in most cases (as here) the centre portion was heightened for electrification. The overbridges of 1838/9 between Stratford and Brentwood were also to this design, but these all went with the line widenings.

Bridge 200 (Wagstaff's Bridge) at Abbots Hall Farm, Stanway (GR 944252) shows the basic design of the original three-arch overbridges with segmental arches, however in this case everything above the arches was reconstructed in engineering bricks in the early twentieth century.

below

'Seven Arch Bridge' carrying Seven Arches Road / Hartswood Road over the cutting at Brentwood is well known. The laying of the foundation stone was deemed worthy of a ceremony on 9th July 1842. The bridge was far from complete when the line opened in March 1843. It is 255ft long and 48ft 6in high, and has survived thanks to its height. The middle arch is three-centred, of 34ft span, and the other arches semicircular, of 21ft span. The first, second, fifth, and sixth piers have relieving arches, but the two centre piers do not. The bridge is built in variable bricks, mostly yellow. It was reported that many came second-hand from Old Mill Green House near Ingatestone which was demolished for the railway. In this view showing repairs in 1919 the bridge is clearly still in fair condition, but it has been heavily tied since. When the line was quadrupled the extra two tracks were laid through the third and fifth arches.

The huts in the foreground were for postmen in connection with the Travelling Post Office trains.

COLCHESTER LINE STATIONS

left

The earliest surviving Eastern Counties Railway buildings on the Colchester line are the down side buildings at Brentwood, part of the 'permanent' station built in 1845 to replace the 1840 temporary station. The much more splendid 1845 main building on the up side was demolished in 1932 for the quadrupling. The down side buildings are in red brick with yellow brick dressings; the doorways all have pointed arches.

The plans for the station were approved in April 1845, and may have been one of the last works of Sancton Wood for the ECR, but there is no contemporary reference as to the architect.

The photograph dates from 1931. The little canopy above the entrance was added in 1884 and has since been removed, otherwise these buildings remain largely unaltered today.

The second Ingatestone station off Hall Lane opened in 1844, but the present building in Tudoresque style was not built until 1846. The date appears in the diaperwork in the main gable. (The diaperwork generally is more charming than skilful!). The architect is not known. Lord Petre's 1840 replacement Almshouses are in the same style, so it may be that Petre pushed the ECR to adopt this style for the station. The leftmost few feet as seen here are an extension of c1890, without diaperwork. Ingatestone retains that now very rare thing an unmodernised Booking Hall; the timber Booking Office screen is believed to date from 1872. There is also a Waiting Room with original fireplace.

A small crossing keeper's cottage was built in the same style (p.53).

The up platform had only a shelter originally. In 1885 a range of Domestic Revival buildings was provided on the up side (p30).

THE CAMBRIDGE LINE

The Cambridge line is quite different from the Colchester line; apart from the enforced tunnelling at Audley End, it follows the river valleys throughout, and thus lacks major bridgeworks, and has few road underbridges. Additionally almost all the overbridges were rebuilt for electrification.

In contrast, it does retain (on its Essex section) many of the original 1840s station buildings. The N&ER had a very mixed bag of station buildings, of which Roydon and Harlow survive, as do the three identical station houses at Stansted, Elsenham and Newport. Robert Stephenson had been the N&ER's Engineer since 1839, but it is not known who designed the station buildings.

Stephenson was also appointed by the ECR as Engineer for the Newport-Brandon 'Extension'. Here he had to work with the ECR's architect Sancton Wood, who designed the fine 1845 buildings at Audley End and Great Chesterford, and probably also the second (1845) Bishops Stortford station (whose main block remains). However, Sancton Wood was really a 'Braithwaite man', and seems to have faded out of active involvement with the ECR some time before he was formally disposed of by the Board in October 1845. Francis Thompson was brought in by Stephenson to finish off the Cambridge line stations, and got much of the credit for them when the line opened.

below

The unique N&ER station building at Roydon almost certainly dates from the opening of the line in 1841 (there is no specific evidence, and the company minutes are lost; but it is already present in an 1843 plan). This 1900s view shows the original character of the building, which was most likely designed this way because of its position directly opposite the entrance lodges to the Briggens estate. The building, now a restaurant, is not fundamentally changed today, but valancing was added to the verandah c1920, giving a much more railway-like feel. To the left of the main section is the tiny station master's house (since given a lean-to roof), and at left we see the 1876 signal box which still exists but has been so much altered as to have no merit.

SANCTON WOOD

Sancton Wood (1816-1886) was appointed as Architect to the ECR under Braithwaite's influence. It was unfortunate that none of his original Colchester line buildings had a long life. In the mid-1840s he worked for several other companies as well as on the ECR's Cambridge line. His principal work in East Anglia was the 1847 station at Bury St Edmunds.

FRANCIS THOMPSON

Francis Thompson (1808-1895) was born in Woodbridge. His father was the County Surveyor of Suffolk, and other close relatives were builders and architects. He learnt via the family and had no formal architectural training. From 1830 to 1838 he lived in Montreal practising as a surveyor and architect. He became acquainted somehow with Robert Stephenson and returned to England to act as architect for Stephenson's North Midland Railway in 1839-42. The Midland Hotel at Derby, and Wingfield station, are the best of the few surviving examples of his work there. The Eastern Counties work was a shortlived job obtained via Stephenson, prior to his receiving a more important commission as architect for Stephenson's Chester & Holyhead line, opened in 1848. His large station at Chester survives largely intact, as do several of the smaller stations, some of which show a clear descent from the Audley End / Great Chesterford plan. Thompson returned to Montreal 1853-59, as architect to the Grand Trunk Railway. His retirement years were spent in Hastings and latterly back at Bredfield near Woodbridge.

left
Harlow Mill in 1965. The right hand pavilion almost certainly had a shaped gable originally. Like Roydon this building is shown on the 1843 plans and can therefore be assumed to date from 1841. Today only the left-hand end of the building remains, cut short at the entrance porch, and in a very sorry state.
Gordon Biddle

bottom left
The 1845 station house cum Booking Office at Elsenham in a contemporary illustration. There is no full proof that these houses were designed for the N&ER, however the fact that they are found only on the N&ER-promoted section of the line beyond Bishops Stortford is fairly conclusive.

bottom right
This 1982 view shows little change, save for the extension of the house on the west side, and the shop. The building remains in this form today but is now neglected. The house is built in a reddish-brown brick with a brighter red brick for the dressings (whereas the houses at Stansted and Newport are in red brick with white brick dressings).

right middle
The 1845 house at Stansted is built gable-to-track, and carries ECR 1850s type canopy brackets (roofing altered). This house was extended considerably in the same style. The flat-arch windows of these houses are well seen here.

right and below

Audley End is generally regarded as the finest of the 1845 Sancton Wood/Thompson Cambridge line stations. The main block is two-storey in buff brick, with a low-pitched hipped roof (invisible from ground level) and semicircular-arched radially-glazed windows. Single-storey blocks at the north and south ends have flat roofing which forms a continuous 'apron' with the verandahs on the platform and road sides. The porte-cochere in rusticated stonework is virtually a separate structure. Photographs 1955.

Gordon Biddle.

below

Great Chesterford is very much in the same spirit as Audley End, also in buff brick, but the building is longer and the windows are all square-headed. This 1955 view shows the verandah on the road side which was unfortunately removed a few years later. The platform verandah, which is still in situ, is similarly supported by diagonal timber struts terminating in pendants (the latter mostly now broken off).

Gordon Biddle.

The south portal of Audley End Tunnel, bearing the arms of Lord Braybrooke of Audley End house on its keystone. The semicircular arches spring from rusticated stone plinths. The ring of bosses features Tudor roses and portcullises alternately. There are five courses of red brick between this ring and the main rusticated stone arch.

Littlebury tunnel south portal is in 'Egyptian' style; the north portals of both tunnels are plain. Sancton Wood may have prepared the portal designs for Stephenson.

THE MALDON AND BRAINTREE BRANCHES

The only other lines built by the ECR in Essex in the 1840s were those from Witham to Braintree and Maldon, opened in 1848. They had been promoted by an independent company, the Maldon Witham & Braintree Railway, which was taken over by the ECR before construction began. The grand Jacobean terminus at Maldon is well-known, but the station and crossing houses elsewhere on these lines were also notable in their way. Only the 'temporary' wooden shack terminus at Braintree let the show down. The architect is not known; it may have been Henry A. Hunt who was appointed as ECR architect in October 1845 when Sancton Wood was given notice. His main work was on the Peterborough and St Ives lines.

THE LOUGHTON BRANCH

The ECR spent most of its resources on damaging and then taking over other companies, and on mismanagement and corruption; and had little to spare for building further new lines itself. Its only new line in Essex after 1848 was the Stratford – Loughton branch opened in 1856. The surviving original buildings on this line are now in Greater London, save for the 1856 Buckhurst Hill station house which now serves as London Underground offices.

below
The 1848 station house at Wickham Bishops, seen here in 1957, was built in half-timbered, almost *cottage orne*, style. It still exists in this form but is not publicly accessible. The house at Cressing was identical but has recently been 'improved' in so horrendous a fashion that it is best not viewed by the sensitive.

The crossing houses at Maldon (Fullbridge) and White Notley (where there was no station originally) were also a 'pair', but brick-built and in a quite different style. Only the White Notley house survives and it too has been modernised in recent years.

Gordon Biddle.

Maldon (East) (situated at GR 853074) was built in 1847/8. The oft-repeated tale that it was made so large in order to prolong work beyond the July 1847 election, at which David Waddington of the ECR was a candidate, is not very likely, as the site for the station was not chosen until March 1847. Real labourers did not have the vote at this date anyway! The true story was that some of the more impoverished of the Maldon electors were paid to 'work' on the railway as a bribe, but as they were not expected to do any real work there would have been no point in enlarging the building.

The building is in red brick with white brick dressings, except for the front arcade and balustrade which are wholly in white brick. The ground floor has semicircular-arched windows with radial glazing, the upper floor has flat-arched windows. There were originally multiple stone finials on the roofline, and along the balustrade. The sections of the balustrade between the brick pillars are single iron castings, painted white.

After several failed episodes since closure, the building is now in good condition again as offices.

If H.A. Hunt was responsible here, it can be seen as a parallel to his Jacobean stations on the North Staffordshire line.

Whilst money seems to have been no object with the Maldon line's stations, it had in contrast several cheaply-built timber viaducts/underbridges, an all too common feature of lines built in East Anglia in the 1840s. Most of these bridges needed heavy repairs within ten years, and on other lines almost all were subsequently replaced by iron bridges. But some of those on the Maldon line soldiered on until closure, as the traffic could readily be worked by light locomotives. The two largest were the viaducts at Wickham Bishops, which lingered long enough after closure to be made an 'Ancient Monument' (!) , and were restored by Essex County Council in 1995. The other timber bridges on the line have now been removed.

The northern or Mill Stream viaduct was originally some 500ft long but was reduced to 150ft (10 spans) in LNER days, the rest becoming an embankment. The southern or River viaduct is 160ft long (12 spans). Both were originally built for double track, but were reduced in width after the line was singled in 1854, probably in 1860 when major repairs were effected. They have a non-symmetrical cross-section in consequence. A public footpath passes under the Mill Stream viaduct at GR 824118.

In this 1958 scene a train from Maldon is seen on the River Viaduct.

Frank Church

CHAPTER TWO

PETER BRUFF AND FREDERICK BARNES: THE EASTERN UNION AND TENDRING HUNDRED RAILWAYS

The railways of northeast Essex, including most of the station buildings surviving today, were not built by the ECR (which never built beyond Colchester) but by the Eastern Union Railway and the Tendring Hundred Railway, to both of which Peter Bruff was Engineer.

THE EASTERN UNION RAILWAY

Very little remains today of the original 1846 infrastructure on the Colchester – Ipswich section. The original station buildings at Ardleigh and Manningtree are long gone (the red brick station house at Ardleigh was built by the GER in 1865). The over-bridges were almost all rebuilt for electrification in the 1980s, and only a couple of underbridges remain in original state.

THE SUDBURY BRANCH

In contrast the 1849 Marks Tey – Sudbury line, promoted by the Colchester Stour Valley Sudbury & Halstead Railway but for practical purposes part of the EUR, features Bruff's greatest work, the Chappel viaduct. It had been intended to build a timber viaduct here but Bruff changed his mind after considering the likely future maintenance costs. When he delivered a paper on the viaduct to the Institution of Civil Engineers in 1850 and spoke of the low cost of the brick viaduct (£21,000), that great advocate of timber construction I.K.Brunel retorted that a timber viaduct would have been cheaper still!

Built for double track, the viaduct has a total length of 1136ft and a maximum height from foundations to rail level of 80ft. There are 32 semicircular arches of 30ft span. The line is on a 1 in 120 gradient rising from south to north; each arch has a springing point 3.5in above the previous arch, giving a total rise of 9ft 6in. The contractor George Wythes (who also built the Hadleigh and Harwich lines) managed to find good brick earth nearby so all the bricks could be made locally. Eighteen of the piers are on mass-concrete foundations but the others have only brick footings as the ground conditions were unusually good. Construction began in July 1847, with completion early in 1849.

Most of the other original over- and under-bridges remain on this line. The only original station in Essex was Bures but the elegant building there was demolished in the 1970s. (For Chappel station see p.36). The crossing house at Mount Bures survives (p.53).

PETER BRUFF

Peter Schuyler Bruff (1812-1900) had trained under Joseph Locke, and later worked under Braithwaite on the ECR until sacked in 1842. This however did little harm to his career. He moved to Ipswich, where he lived until his death, and became both a leading promoter of and Engineer to the Eastern Union and Ipswich & Bury Railways, which opened the Colchester – Ipswich – Bury lines in 1846. The EUR and Bruff then went on to build the line to Norwich (1849) and, via associated companies, the branches from Bentley to Hadleigh (1847), Marks Tey to Sudbury (1849), and Manningtree to Harwich (1854). After the EUR was taken over by the ECR in 1854, Bruff was appointed ECR Engineer until resigning in 1857, but this time was spent in repairing decaying 1840s structures rather than on new works.

By this date he was also acting as Engineer to the Waveney Valley Railway, which opened the line from Tivetshall to Beccles in stages in 1855-63; and to the grandly-named Norwich & Spalding Railway, whose line from Spalding to Sutton Bridge opened in two sections in 1858/62. Bruff's involvement here, outside his usual territory, was due to the EUR directors being heavily involved with the company.

The later decades of Bruff's life were focused on Tendring where in addition to building the railways he also became the chief influence on property developments. In 1855 he purchased a large area of land immediately south of Walton town centre, which he partly developed in 1859-63 with housing and the Clifton Hotel. The Tendring Hundred Railway, opened from Hythe to Walton in 1863-7, was seen as a further necessary step in reviving Walton's fortunes.

However even before the railway opened to Walton Bruff had largely transferred his development affections to Clacton which, as a virgin site, was seen as having more potential. He bought a large estate here in 1865 and development began in the early 1870s. An initial attempt to build a railway failed, but a second attempt saw the Clacton-on-Sea Railway open the branch from Thorpe in 1882, inevitably with Bruff as Engineer.

above

The official ceremony for the start of work on Chappel viaduct took place on 14th September 1847, when this stone was laid. Note the spelling 'Chapple'. The CSVS&HR had already been leased to the EUR by the time work began.

right middle

The viaduct is built entirely in brick (in English bond), with no use of stone and no decorative elements, relying on proportion alone for its aesthetics. Bruff called the bricks 'grey' but they are more reddish-brown. They must have been of good quality as, in great contrast to the 1842 main line viaducts, there has been little need for patching. The arches are of six rings, and there is a three-course string course immediately above. The imposts are in three sections of four, three, and two courses.

top right

All the piers have a 6ft-wide central opening, varying in height according to the height of the pier, with a three-course semicircular arch at the top and a two-course semi-circular arch at the bottom. More unusually, there are also (invisible) 'voids' in the piers either side of the central opening, 4ft by 3ft at the bottom tapering towards the top.

bottom right

Bridge 881 on the Sudbury line at GR 898263 carries Moor Rd / Tey Rd over the line with a single long segmental flying arch springing from the embankment sides. The arch is of six rings, the outer two standing proud. The other overbridges on the line have three-centred arches.

THE HARWICH BRANCH

This line, another child of the EUR, was opened in 1854 and featured some very attractive station buildings, of which Mistley and Dovercourt survive. They were probably designed by Bruff's favoured architect Frederick Barnes.

Following the estuary as it does, the line has no major bridge-works. Half a dozen of the original underbridges remain, and two original overbridges at Manningtree. The other overbridges were rebuilt for electrification in the 1980s.

FREDERICK BARNES

Frederick Barnes (1814-1898) had moved to Ipswich in 1843 to assist with the building of the new Customs House, and his railway career began when Bruff used him as architect for the Ipswich & Bury line whose Jacobean-style stations of 1846/7 were amongst the most flamboyant ever built in this country. Those at Needham Market, Stowmarket, and Thurston survive. Barnes also designed the Hadleigh branch stations (of which Raydon Wood and Hadleigh remain) and the stations on the Norwich line (of which only Diss survives). The Norwich line buildings were much less grandiose as the country was in a financial crisis by 1848/9. From 1850 Barnes was in general practice in Ipswich, specialising in churches, chapels and school buildings. Bruff (almost certainly) used him again for the Harwich branch stations, the Waveney Valley line stations in 1855 and 1863, and the Tendring Hundred Railway stations.

[It should however be noted that the only hard specific evidence for Barnes being involved on the last three lines relates purely to Hadleigh and Walton stations. It seems very unlikely in the circumstances that he did not also design the other Hadleigh branch stations at Capel and Raydon Wood. As Walton (though necessarily very different in layout, as a terminus) shares so many features with the other THR stations, it would seem highly likely that Barnes was responsible for them too, in which case he would also have been responsible for the Waveney Valley stations from which they were copied. See also further comment in the captions here.]

left upper and lower
The 1854 Harwich line stations were built to Italianate designs. Mistley, the most attractive, is in red brick with white gault brick dressings, and has recently been cleaned and restored. Two pairs of pilasters rise to broken-pedimented gables. The semicircular-arched windows with radial glazing had been used previously by Barnes on the Hadleigh branch stations and became a trademark of his (although many other architects also used them, cf Audley End). Top photograph 1981.

In 1855 the station at Harleston on the Waveney Valley line was built to a somewhat more elaborate version of the Mistley design.

below
A platform view of Mistley c1900. The main building was much plainer on this side. If one ignores for a moment the station's horses, children, and goat, the main point of interest on this side is the central open waiting area flanked by single-storey blocks. This was to become another Bruff / Barnes trademark, reappearing in the standard Waveney Valley / Tendring Hundred stations; but the triangular-plan bay windows in the station offices, provided to give a view up and down the line without leaving the office, were not repeated after the Harwich line. For the 1882 Mistley signal box see p.68.

16

To the modern eye Dovercourt is probably a less attractive ensemble. Again it is in red brick with gault brick dressings. The two projecting porches are wholly in gault brick, and the pediment in stone. The platform side of this building was much altered when a full-length canopy was provided in 1882 (p.42). Photograph 1973.

J.E. Connor

Wrabness was demolished in the 1980s but this photograph is included to show how the Harwich branch stations formed a family group. (The fourth station, Harwich, was timber-built and only lasted till 1865). Wrabness was wholly in red brick and its principal features were the large recessed areas and the heavy string course rising in a semicircular arch over the main entrance.

The best-preserved of the 1854 bridges on the Harwich line is this underbridge No.1056 at Shore Lane, Bradfield (GR 144313). It is a skew bridge in red brick, with a four-ring white brick segmental arch, end pilasters, and curving wing walls. The bridges were built for double track and therefore did not need altering when the line was doubled in 1882. Other underbridges surviving in reasonably original condition and readily accessible are Manningtree Station Rd (GR 100321), the accommodation bridge at GR 151313 (photo p.3), and the 'tunnel' at GR 187316.

THE TENDRING HUNDRED RAILWAY

This was a completely independent company, with Bruff as Engineer. Six of the stations (Hythe, 1863; Wivenhoe, 1863; Alresford, 1866; Great Bentley, 1866; Weeley, 1866; and Kirby Cross, 1866) had buildings to a standard design copied from the Waveney Valley line stations in Norfolk, and probably to be attributed to Barnes. Wivenhoe was demolished in 1886 but the other five survive, mostly in a neglected state.

St Botolph's, Thorpe-le-Soken, and Walton were variations on the theme, as described in the captions here.

In contrast Thorington station building (demolished), and Frinton gatehouse, were copies of a very different design evolved by Bruff for the Norwich & Spalding Railway.

The THR had no major bridgeworks, the countryside being flat. Nothing of substance remains from the 1860s except the three-arch overbridge at Alresford Road (GR 052215).

THE CLACTON-ON-SEA RAILWAY

Another independent company was formed to build the short Thorpe-le-Soken to Clacton line, opened in 1882. The original Clacton station, a timber building of rather un-railwaylike appearance, was demolished in 1929 when the present station was built, and no other original works of substance remain.

left
Starston, one of the three identical 1855 stations on the Waveney Valley Railway that formed the model for most of the Tendring Hundred Railway stations. The others were Pulham Market and Pulham St Mary. The 1860 stations on the middle part of the WVR line were quite different (see p.20, caption to Frinton photograph), but the 1855 design was revived for Ditchingham, Ellingham and Geldeston in 1863.

In fact there are some differences between the 1855 WVR stations on the one hand, and the 1863 WVR stations and the THR stations on the other hand. The 1855 stations have a second white brick string course just below eaves level, curving above the first floor end windows as seen here; and the brickwork of the arch above the main road side entrance porch stands a little proud of the rest, with a brick 'keystone'.

*Douglas Thompson /
Stations UK*

bottom left
The greater part of Barnes' 1867 Walton station (the last station building to be designed by him) still remains, however the recent residential conversion has involved changes such that an overall view is no longer appropriate. Also, the west end of the building was demolished by a runaway train in 1987, and a pastiche reconstruction has been provided in lieu. This detail shows a typical 'Barnes' window in an unaltered section of the north front.

below
The real oddity amongst the THR stations is Thorpe-le-Soken; there is no evident reason why a standard building could not have been erected here. This unique building nevertheless has several common features with the standard type – on the road side the white brick 'quoins' and string course, on the platform side a virtually 'standard' waiting area with single-storey blocks at either end (but with simple lean-to roofing, and valancing). The building was nicely restored in 2004/5 after being derelict for some years. Photograph 1981.

A 1900s view of Alresford. On both the WVR and the THR, these stations were built in red brick with white gault brick dressings (except that the first floor windows in the end walls, and the windows on the platform side of the single-storey blocks at either end of the waiting area, had red brick surrounds). The alternating three-course gault brick 'quoins' are a conspicuous feature. All the windows in the main part of the building were of the semicircular-arched / radial glazed type. The single-storey ancillary buildings at right were a standard original feature of all the THR stations of this type.

As ever, there are minor variations in the details of the brickwork at these theoretically-'standard' stations, notably in the string course, and in the area between the head of the arch above the porch and the dentillation above.

The Lens of Sutton Collection

A period view of the platform side of Weeley station. The arrangement of the open waiting area at the WVR / THR stations, whilst the same in principle as at Mistley, is somewhat different in details. Weeley is now boarded up and empty but remains the least altered of the five surviving THR station houses of this type.

The Lens of Sutton Collection

St Botolph's (now Colchester Town) station, opened in 1866, could not have had one of the standard buildings owing to its peculiarly-constricted site. At first it strikes one as little-related to the standard type, but one must remove from one's thoughts the canopy, which was added by the GER in 1884 (p.43). The 'Barnes' windows on the ground floor then stand out more clearly (those on the front have been altered since this 1954 photograph, but those at the rear remain). The first-floor windows may have been made flat-arched to harmonise better with the Georgian house at left which had been bought by the THR to serve as its offices and Boardroom, later becoming the station master's house. The 1866 building here is also in a brighter red brick than the other THR stations, again probably to match the older house (no join can be seen in the brickwork at the rear). We may guess that Barnes was responsible for the design here but again there is no specific evidence.

The platform canopy glimpsed at right probably dated back to 1866; it still exists in principle but much of what is there now belongs to a 1991 'restoration'.

Gordon Biddle.

were the stations at Redenhall Wortwell and Earsham on the Waveney Valley's 1860 section. These very plain gabled houses, with the conspicuously-dentillated brickwork at eaves level the only 'feature', are very 1860s in their ambience, and one suspects they were designed by Bruff himself for cheapness.

left
Frinton gatehouse (1867) is a direct copy of the 1858/62 gatehouses between Spalding and Sutton Bridge on the Bruff-engineered Norwich & Spalding Railway. The N&S station buildings at Whaplode and Weston were also to this design, as

right
A recent view of Norwich & Spalding gatehouse No.86 near Gedney. Even the little canopy above the door is exactly the same as at Frinton!

Nigel Digby

We end this chapter with brief reference to two small independent companies that became part of the GER system later.

above
This is the Saffron Walden Railway's 1865 Saffron Walden station, almost certainly designed by the company's Engineer John Sampson Pierce. It has recently been converted to two houses, with a new canopy added on the 'platform' side. Photograph July 1963.

John Watling

left
There is precious little left from the Wivenhoe & Brightlingsea Railway's structures (although the whole of the trackbed remains intact). One pair of cylinders on each bank are all that is left of its Alresford Swing Bridge, built in 1864/5 by Shaws of Birmingham under the WVR Engineers James S. Cooke and J. Olroyd Greaves, and dismantled in 1967. In the background of this view is the boatshed built by the LNER to accommodate the rowing boat that the bridgemen needed to convey them to/from the bridge when open. (GR 059198).

CHAPTER THREE

THE GREAT EASTERN RAILWAY 1862 – 1883
with a feature on Harwich

NEW LINES 1862 – 1868

The newly-formed Great Eastern Railway (incorporated 1862 as an amalgamation of the Eastern Counties and most of the other lines in East Anglia) began its architectural life with a strong burst of standardisation on the new lines built in Essex and Suffolk in 1862-66: Loughton to Ongar, Bishops Stortford to Braintree, Sudbury – Haverhill – Shelford, and Long Melford to Bury St Edmunds. The construction of these lines was entrusted to a 'New Lines Department' in the GER Engineer's office, and Robert Sinclair, the ECR/GER Engineer 1857-66, had personal charge of them. The station buildings must therefore be attributed to him, but we will never know how much of the architectural design was done by his understaff. The standardised buildings, which have become known as the '1865 type', all had the same two-storey hipped-roof station master's house section, but the station offices came in large medium and small versions according to the importance of the place (see captions for details). Twelve of the 27 new stations on these lines come within the area covered by this book:

	Size	brickwork
Loughton	large	not known (Demolished)
Debden	small	all white (House only remains)
Theydon Bois	medium	red with white dressings
Epping	large	all red
North Weald	small	all red
Blake Hall	small	red with white dressings
Ongar	large	red with white dressings
Takeley	small	all white
Dunmow	medium	red with white dressings (Demol.)
Felsted	small	red with white dressings
Rayne	small	red with white dressings
Braintree	large	red with white dressings

All the above were built in 1864-6, although the Bishops Stortford – Braintree line did not actually open until 1869. The design was also used for new buildings at two stations on existing lines, Marks Tey in 1864 (mostly demolished) and Finningham in 1865 (Suffolk, demolished).

There was also a standard '1865' single-storey block which was used as the sole building at the smallest stations (Glemsford, Cockfield, Bury Eastgate) and as the 'other platform' waiting rooms block at the larger two-platform stations. Epping and Theydon Bois still have them although much altered.

During Sinclair's subsequent period as Consulting Engineer for new lines only (1866-8) there were not actually any new lines completed, as this coincided with the GER's worst financial crisis period.

ROBERT SINCLAIR

Robert Sinclair (1816-1898), the first of three Scotsmen who were to engineer most of the extensions of the GER system from 1857 to 1910, was, like many of his generation, both a mechanical and a civil engineer. The son of Alexander Sinclair, a prominent London-based merchant, he was educated at Charterhouse and then apprenticed to Messrs Scott Sinclair & Co. of Greenock, his uncle Robert being a member of the firm. After working on the Liverpool & Manchester and Grand Junction Railways, he became Locomotive Superintendent of the Glasgow Paisley & Greenock Railway in 1844. This led to the posts of Locomotive Superintendent (1847) and Engineer (1851) of the Caledonian Railway. He came to the ECR as Locomotive Superintendent in 1856, and was made Engineer also in 1857 when Bruff resigned. From 1862 he continued in these posts for the GER, until May 1866. He then set himself up as a Consulting Engineer in London, continuing to work for the GER on new lines only 1866-8; but was forced to give up work in 1868, at the age of 51, owing to bad health. After a period in Devon, he spent the rest of his life in Rome and Tuscany, pursuing literary interests including a translation of Dante. He died in Florence on 20th October 1898.

An Edwardian view of the '1865' 'small' type station at Blake Hall, showing the arrangement of the main (garden) frontage of the station house that was common to all three sizes of '1865' station. Closed 25 years ago, this station remains intact as a private house.

top

Rayne illustrates the platform side of the 'small' version of the '1865' stations. This building is 'handed' the opposite way to Blake Hall. The single-storey section with the Booking Hall/Booking Office has a half-hip roof at the end opposite the house, and the eaves are continued down to form a small canopy on the platform side, supported on 36in by 24in iron brackets. The Gents (right) is a reconstruction of 1994 when Rayne station was restored as an information centre for the 'Flitch Way'. The stations on the Bishops Stortford – Braintree line, unlike those on the other '1865' lines, have painted stucco surrounds to the windows and doors, perhaps an improvement that came as a result of their being the last stations of this type to be built, in 1865/6.

This station is at GR 726224.

middle

Another view of Rayne showing the architectural details better. The conspicuous 'quoins' are formed of four courses each (the topmost one of three courses), a little proud of the other brickwork. There are three two-course string courses (immediately under the eaves, at first floor level, and level with the top of the ground floor windows). All these dressings are highlighted here by being in white gault brick in contrast to the red brick of the rest.

The section of the building at left was an extension of c1901. The usual cause of these not uncommon station house extensions was the station master and wife producing too many children – a factor which had nearly as much influence on the building history of country stations as traffic considerations! The extension kept faithfully to the original style, except that for some unfathomable reason the 'quoins' were omitted on the corner seen here.

bottom left

This 1960s view of Blake Hall shows the road side arrangement of the '1865' 'small' station building.

J.E. Connor

bottom right

Theydon Bois, the only remaining 'medium' size '1865' station in Essex, had alterations effected when London Transport took over, including bricking in part of the roadside canopy area. Photograph 1975.

above

The 'medium' and 'large' versions of the '1865' stations had a single-storey central link section (fronted by a canopy on the road side) and a single-storey hipped pavilion at the far end. The central link section was longer in the 'large' version.

This is Ongar, the least altered of the remaining 'large' '1865' stations in Essex.

bottom left

Detail of the Booking Hall entrance at Braintree, everything seen here being in near-original condition. These brackets on the road side are timber.

right middle

The Booking Office screen and ticket window at Ongar, a rare survival.

bottom right

A point that has not been emphasised before is that the first '1865' style station built was Marks Tey, on an existing line. It was designed by/in 1863, as the contract was let in November 1863 and work was completed in summer 1864. (It is however still possible that the design had been drawn up principally with the new lines in mind). The main (up side) building at Marks Tey was demolished in the 1970s but this unique 1865-style building on the down island platform remains. It is in white brick.

At Easton Lodge, between Takeley and Dunmow (GR 603213), a crossing house was built in the '1865' style. It is to cheaper dimensions than the station masters' houses; the ceilings are lower on both floors, and there are only two string courses. It is built in white gault brick and has the same painted stucco window surrounds as the stations on this line (but not for the door). The porch is no doubt a later addition but it makes for a charming composition. At right is the former ground frame hut, probably of c1920.

A similar '1865' crossing house survives at Glemsford, a few yards beyond the Essex county boundary.

Standardised bridge designs were also used on the '1865' lines. This is bridge No.2095 east of Rayne (GR 731225), one of seven examples of this type of overbridge that can be studied from the 'Flitch Way' railway path. In accordance with normal practice they were built for double track, although this line remained single in the event. All are in English bond, those at the west end of the line in white brick, those at the eastern end in red brick. All have five-ring three-centred arches, but the details of the brickwork above the arch are not actually identical. The parapet walls have a coping of blue bullnosed bricks, some of which are marked 'Hamblet Oldbury near Birmingham' and dated '1865'.

Most of the road underbridges on this line were iron girder spans on brick abutments; replacement spans were installed in 1894/5 for heavier trains.

NEW LINES 1868 – 1883

With the exception of the short Parkeston loop, all the new lines built by the GER in this period were outside Essex. However, we must look at the work done in these years, both because it brought into our story the two most important figures of later years, and to avoid a gap in our account of the development of GER architecture.

When Sinclair retired in 1868 the GER appointed the Consulting Engineer Edward Wilson to take charge of the new lines being promoted in London in connection with the Liverpool Street extension. Under Wilson GER architecture moved into a Gothic phase, for the stations on the new lines from Bethnal Green to Edmonton and Walthamstow (opened 1870-3) and most famously of course at Liverpool Street (opened 1874/5). However, no stations were built in this style in present-day Essex. Wilson died in 1877 but his firm Edward Wilson & Co. continued to act as the GER's 'Consulting and Constructing Engineers' for most new lines up to the Mildenhall branch opened in 1884/5, this including the parliamentary work. Most of the GER work was done by John Wilson and Neville Ashbee, who subsequently went on to the GER staff, as Engineer and architect respectively, in 1883, as described in Chapter 4.

EDWARD WILSON

Edward Wilson (1820-1877) was like Sinclair both a locomotive and civil engineer. Brought up near Edinburgh, he worked first under his civil engineer father, and was then articled to the mechanical engineers Messrs Stark & Fulton of Glasgow. After working on the Caledonian Canal and several railways, he became Engineer to the York & North Midland Railway in 1847, and then to the Midland Great Western Railway of Ireland from 1853. From 1858 he was Locomotive and Permanent Way Engineer to the Oxford Worcester & Wolverhampton (later West Midland) Railway, until the company was taken over by the GWR.

In 1864 he set himself up in London as a Consulting Engineer, and worked on the Metropolitan Railway's Moorgate–Liverpool St section, and on several new GWR lines, as well as on the extensive GER projects.

Wilson was a modest man and his early death in August 1877 prevented him from gaining a greater reputation. He was described as 'one of the most unobtrusive but painstaking and hardworking of our railway engineers'. The Edward Wilson & Co. firm continued after his death as a partnership between John Wilson and J.S.Macintyre.

NEW STATIONS ON EXISTING GER LINES 1862 –1883

All new works on existing GER lines in this period were done in-house by the GER Engineer's department, so that, except under Sinclair 1862-6, the men responsible were entirely different from those responsible for the new lines in this period. The GER Engineers after Sinclair were Henry W. Davis 1866-73, and Alfred A.Langley who came from the LSWR in 1873 and resigned in 1883. There are no known references to any architect being involved. There is little evident pattern in the new station buildings erected on existing lines under the Sinclair Davis and Langley regimes. The surviving examples in Essex are Harwich (1866), Hatfield Peverel (1878), and Newport (designed c1879, erected c1884), all of which are illustrated here.

top right
Exterior view of the second Harwich station, which was completed in summer 1866. It has definite '1865' connections, *vide* the quoins and some of the windows, but is otherwise unique. It must be attributed to Sinclair's office. The use of bay windows like this in a station building is unusual. The whole building is in white gault brick. There was originally an east-west wing at the north end incorporating the station master's house, now demolished. The short remaining section of platform canopy was heavily rebuilt in the 1980s.

second right
Hatfield Peverel had been without a station for many years until the GER Board agreed to provide a new station in 1876. The contract was given to C.Lewis in September 1877 at £1,104, and the station opened in 1878. Alfred Langley's office must have been responsible for the design which is quite different from any other GER station. The building is in yellow brick with bright red brick dressings, including a three-course band of red brick level with the top of the ground floor windows, and another of one course level with the cill of the first floor windows. The overall effect is pleasant enough and the building remains in good condition.

third right
Newport was the last station built in Essex to a 'pre-Ashbee' design. The complete remodelling of the station and track layout, in connection with the abolition of the level crossing, was authorised in December 1879 at the very large estimate of £6,800. However progress was slow; a November 1883 plan shows the level crossing still in situ.

The new station buildings, probably designed in 1879, were commodious enough but were quite plain, with flat arch windows, and unimpressive from the road side as the 1845 station house was retained and most of the new down side block was hidden behind it. The Booking Office, seen here, was at the south end, on the alignment of the closed road over the level crossing. By the time the work was done in 1884/5 Ashbee was firmly in charge so, whilst the basic plans were not altered, the platform canopies received the new standard type valancing. Photograph 1982.

bottom
The down (left) and up side (right) buildings at Newport (see p.44 for details of the canopies).

HARWICH

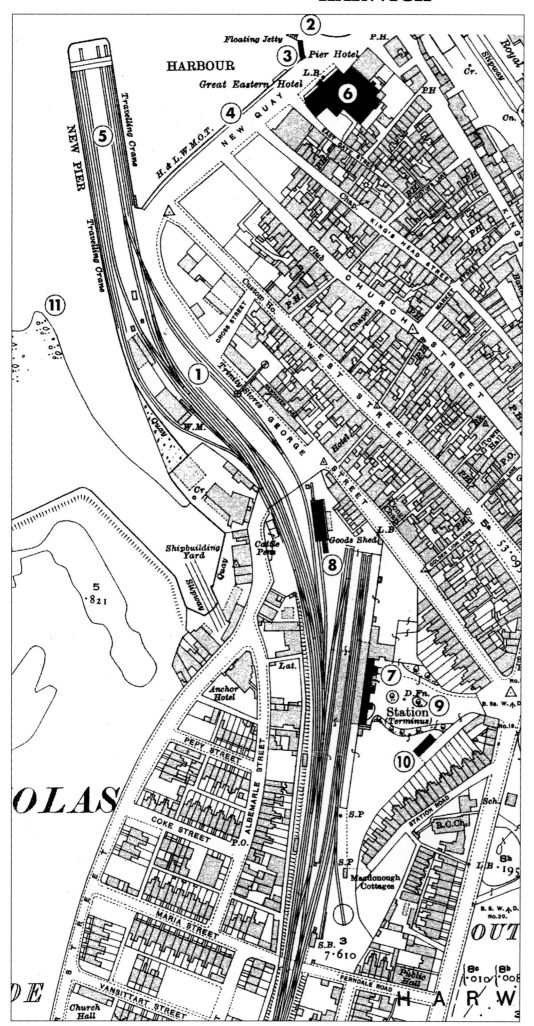

Ordnance Survey 25in map, 1922 survey. Railway buildings extant in 2005 are shaded in black.

1. Site of original Harwich station 1854-1865/6.

2. Halfpenny Pier (alias Town Pier, or Corporation Pier). Built by Harwich Corporation 1852/3, Peter Bruff Engineer. [The greater part of the pier is off the edge of this map sheet]. Used by the ECR/GER ships from 1854. Because the Corporation was unable to repay its loans, the GER gradually acquired a controlling interest in the pier, and it eventually became GER property in 1872 (remaining railway-owned until sold by BR to the Harwich Haven Authority in 1974). Although deserted by the main continental ships after 1865, the Ha'penny Pier continued to be used by the railway's pleasure excursion vessels and Shotley/Felixstowe ferry boats. The seaward end of the pier was burnt out in July 1923 and the remains removed in 1943.

3. Halfpenny Pier Booking Office and Waiting Room, built by the GER in the 1890s. The original 1853 Booking Office here was a two-storey octagonal structure, which seems to have been reconstructed (?) subsequently as a single-storey building with a Waiting Shed attached. The present buildings were then erected on the same site, but the references in the GER minutes are rather confusing.

4. 'New Quay', built 1852/3 by Harwich Corporation as part of the same improvements as the Halfpenny Pier, prior to the arrival of the railway. The previous shoreline is indicated by the limit of the old buildings in Kings Head St and Church St. The New Quay also became GER property in 1872.

5. Continental Pier (alias New Pier, GER Pier, or (latterly) Trinity House Pier). Built by the GER in 1865/6 as a 490ft by 90ft timber pier for use by the principal continental ships, for which the Halfpenny Pier was too small for convenience. Perry & Judson were the contractors. The 1854 passenger station had to be removed because it was in the way of the approaches to this pier. In the event the continental traffic grew so fast after 1865 that the construction of Parkeston Quay had to be authorised in 1874, and after its opening in 1883 the Continental Pier became a secondary facility for some of the cargo ships only. The outer end of the pier was destroyed by a fire in June 1910 and rebuilt in concrete in 1915-21. After the 1939-45 war the pier was taken over by Trinity House for buoy storage. It was narrowed for most of its length in 1957.

6. Great Eastern Hotel (1865). The GER saw a hotel as necessary partly because the continental ships did not operate daily at this period. The first stone was laid in April 1864 and the Hotel opened on 1st June 1865. It lost much of its trade after Parkeston Quay opened, and, after previous temporary closures, was eventually closed for good in 1923. It later became Harwich Town Hall but has now been converted to flats as 'Riverside Court'.

7. Second Harwich station built 1865/6 – see photograph p.25 caption for details.

8. Goods Shed (1865). Built in yellow brick. Now derelict.

9. Drinking fountain, part of landscaping improvements made by the GER to the station yard in 1882.

10. Stables (1913). This six-horse block on the east side of the station yard was built by A.Coe of Ipswich for £436. (See photograph p.67).

11. [Not shown on this map due to its earlier date]. Position of Train Ferry Pier, opened 1924 using second-hand structures built in 1917 for the wartime government train ferries from Southampton and Richborough. The Harwich gantry came from Richborough but the 120ft 'link span' came from Southampton. Disused since the start of Channel Tunnel freight services and now derelict, it is a 'listed building'.

right

The Great Eastern Hotel at Harwich could be said to be the finest surviving railway building in Essex. The Architect was Thomas Allom and the contractors Lucas Bros of Lowestoft. The *Essex Standard* of 2nd June 1865 reported the previous day's celebrations, and noted:

'The elevation is in the Free Italian style, of white Suffolk brick, with stone cornice. The central entrance is by a stone porch with a bold flight of steps. There are arched windows to the ground floor with stone dressings, and intervening medallions (beautifully carved) of ten of the Sovereigns of England, selected chiefly for their connection with the harbour of Harwich. In front of the windows of the first floor, which is chiefly devoted to private sitting rooms and suites of apartments, is a stone balcony, protected by ornamental iron work, running the whole extent of the building. Between the first and second floors is an enriched string course; and between the second floor and the attic storey is a bold ornamental cornice of stone. The windows of the ground floor are composed of pedestals and columns with massive panes and stone cills, the centre of the columns having square dies, neatly carved to imitate sea shells, and each surmounted by a beautiful carved capital in the conventional style........surmounting the centre division of the building is a very massive pediment, containing at present the Royal Arms, but this is intended to give place to a handsome illuminated clock (the gift of Messrs Lucas Bros)'.

The 'principal apartments' consisted of 'a dining hall, two coffee-rooms, two billiard-rooms, seven private sitting-rooms, sixty bed-rooms, smoking room, tavern bar, hotel bar, waiting-room, washing-room, bath rooms, etc'. The ground floor rooms had 15ft ceilings, the first floor 11ft, second floor 10ft, and attic storey 9ft. On top of the roof was 'a lead flat, 60ft by 20ft, enclosed by palisading, for a promenade'.

The building remains in excellent external condition today. The only significant changes are the removal of the string course between the first and second floors, the removal of the ironwork on the second floor balconies, and the disappearance of the hotel name below the pediment.

The rear parts of the building are in unadorned white brick.

Thomas Allom (1804-1872) was apprenticed to the architect Francis Goodwin from 1819 to 1826 and later worked as an architect both on his own account and in association with Sir Charles Barry (including some work on the Houses of Parliament). However he was and is better known for his work as a topographical illustrator, producing prints for books on Europe, Turkey, and the near and far east.

bottom

Detail of the pediment and the attic storey cornice. The clock is surrounded by a laurel wreath and supported by sea monsters with lions' heads.

top left
Details of the ground floor windows and their capitals, the first floor balconies, and two of the royal medallions.

left
Close-up of the entrance porch with its 'swag' decoration.

top right
A recent view of the GER Halfpenny Pier Booking Office and Waiting Room.

JOHN WILSON

JOHN ('Jack') WILSON (1846-1922) was the son of Edward Wilson's brother Robert Wilson of Glasgow. He initially served articles as a mechanical engineer but was then articled to his uncle Edward Wilson as a civil engineer, working on the GER schemes. He soon became a senior figure in the firm, and then partner 1877-83. He acted as Resident Engineer for the East Norfolk Railway. In 1883 the partnership was broken up by agreement to allow him to go on to the GER staff as (Chief) Engineer, a position he retained until retiring in 1910.

Wilson was a popular figure both in the GER and in the London Scottish societies. He married Emily Swarbrick, daughter of the GER General Manager Samuel Swarbrick, and lived in later years at the Clock House (New Place), Upminster. He is buried in Upminster churchyard.

His major works after 1883 were Liverpool Street East side, the main line widening to Romford, and the New Essex lines to Southend/Southminster/Maldon.

NEVILLE ASHBEE

(WILLIAM) NEVILLE ASHBEE (c1852-1919) was articled to Alfred Maberley, the Diocesan Surveyor for Gloucester, 1868-72, and remained in his office until 1874 when he joined Edward Wilson's firm, acting initially as resident architect for the construction of Liverpool Street. From 1876 to 1882 he was 'Assistant in the Architect's Department', and in 1882-3 'Head of the Architectural Department', for Edward Wilson & Co. In these roles he designed most or all of the stations on the new GER lines of those years (cf John Wilson's words in his retirement speech in 1910, 'for all the buildings I have put up for the last 26 years, and for many years previously, I am indebted to Mr Ashbee'). For the last two GER lines built by the Wilson firm, the East Norfolk Railway Western Extension from Wroxham to County School, and the Mildenhall branch, a standard design of station building was evolved. It was also in these years that the standard GER platform canopy design was developed (p.42).

When John Wilson transferred to the GER staff in October 1883, Ashbee went with him to become 'Head of the Architectural Section'. He retained this post until retiring through ill health in April 1916. Ashbee became ARIBA 1881 and FRIBA 1890. His most significant individual station buildings were Norwich Thorpe, Hertford East, Southend (Victoria) (p.34), Colchester (p.39), Felixstowe, and Newmarket.

CHAPTER FOUR

THE GREAT EASTERN RAILWAY 1883 – 1922: ASHBEE DOMESTIC REVIVAL AND BEYOND
with a feature on Chappel

When their Engineer Alfred Langley resigned in 1883 to take up a corresponding post on the Midland Railway, the GER Board decided to make some fundamental changes to their engineering arrangements. By agreement with the Edward Wilson & Co. firm, John Wilson transferred to the GER staff as Chief Engineer as from 1st October 1883, and Neville Ashbee transferred similarly from the same date to be Head of the Architectural Section under Wilson. From this date, therefore, all GER engineering and architectural work, both for new lines and on existing lines, was done by one in-house team (for the first time since 1866). This remained the case until the end of the company's existence in 1922. As Wilson did not retire until 1910, and Ashbee not until 1916, this brought a long period of architectural continuity.

As one would expect in the circumstances, practice after 1883 tended to follow that established by Wilson and Ashbee for new lines prior to 1883. This was particularly noticeable in respect of platform canopies (Chapter 5). However, so far as station buildings went, Ashbee seems to have undergone a conversion to the 'Domestic Revival' style at much the same time as his transfer to the GER, and from the start his post-1883 work bore a quite different feel to what had come before (and in particular bore no relation to the standard stations on the Wroxham - County School and Mildenhall lines). The London Brighton & South Coast Railway had made a big show of the Domestic Revival style in its new 1880-82 lines in Sussex, but the style was still fairly *avant garde* for railway use at this date and Ashbee therefore became a significant proponent of it. With the GER's finances improving at this period, the company was able to undertake more station improvements from the mid 1880s, and shake off the old ECR image of shackery and unpunctuality. From our immediate viewpoint, also, whilst little work had been undertaken in Essex in the 1870s, the county was to see a lot of GER activity in the 1880s.

Ashbee's first months with the GER were heavily dominated by the preparation of plans for what was in the event his *magnum opus*, the new Norwich Thorpe terminus, built 1884-6, for which a Frenchified 'Free Renaissance' style was adopted.

His first small station job after 1883 was the new up side range at Ingatestone (1884/5), and this was the first manifestation of Domestic Revival. Next in Essex were Wivenhoe (1886) and Frinton (1888), both described in detail in the captions here. Cottages and Station Masters' houses also appeared in Domestic Revival style from 1885 (p.50).

There then followed no less than fifteen new stations on the 'New Essex' lines from Shenfield to Southend / Southminster / Maldon, opened in 1888/9 – the biggest railway building project ever undertaken by the GER in Essex. These stations featured a strong element of standardisation in the Domestic Revival style, and at most the buildings were also to one of several common plans. (The exceptions were Billericay and Wickford, the first two built, which one suspects predated the standardisation policy; Maldon West (demolished) where the platforms were in deep cutting and there was only a small Booking Office building at street level; and the Southend terminus). The Southminster line stations proved sadly overlarge for the actual traffic and most of the buildings were demolished in 1968, the only coherent survivals today being parts of Burnham and Southminster. The Southend line

stations are all fully or near-fully extant including canopies, but some are in an unhappy state.

LATER ASHBEE STATIONS

By 1890 the observer might have concluded that Ashbee would continue solely committed to his 1880s Domestic Revival style (albeit this style would not really be appropriate for the largest stations). In the event his 1890s small stations were rather more variable, the only common feature being the use of red brick. Some were in a plainer version of the 1880s style, without the most charming features, the tiled gables and elaborate timber roadside canopies. (Yet as late as 1903 the Lowestoft – Yarmouth line was given a series of lavish stations closely related to the New Essex lines designs, with striped gables; and the Woodford & Ilford line opened in the same year had cottages in pure 1880s style).

Other 1890s stations were quite different in feel, as exemplified by the first two Essex rebuildings of the '90s illustrated here, Chappel and Buckhurst Hill. However it is impossible to attempt any full picture of later Ashbee work here, as the majority of new work was outside Essex.

Subsequent work in Essex was for some years all in the way of rebuildings at major stations - Colchester up side in 1895/6, Chelmsford (partly) in 1898/9, Manningtree in 1898-1900, and Witham in 1906/7. Colchester received an exuberant frontage which must count as the GER's most significant station building anywhere of the 1890s. Manningtree and Witham were fairly plain brick ranges albeit with commodious facilities. Again, these stations are described in full in the photograph captions.

After 1900 the only other new stations in Essex were the Light Railway type wooden buildings on the Kelvedon & Tollesbury line (1904 – all demolished) and the Thaxted branch (1913 – Thaxted survives), plus the new up side Booking Office at Elsenham (p.41).

1880s Ashbee tile-hung gable at Ingatestone.

top

A 1981 view of Ingatestone up side (unfortunately the building is now fenced off on this side and its external condition has deteriorated). The scheme for an additional Booking Office and waiting rooms on the up side was approved by the GER Way & Works Committee on 1st July 1884, and the work was done in 1885. The bright red brick and tile-hung gables were to be replicated in subsequent Ashbee Domestic Revival buildings. It appears from residual marking of the brickwork that there was originally a canopy above the doorway here (as at Wivenhoe).

middle and bottom

Two views of the 1886 station at Wivenhoe, which replaced the 1863 THR buildings when the line was doubled. The contract was given to O.T.Gibbons on 16th March 1886 for £1,850, for completion by 1st July. The main single-storey section here is a near-copy of Ingatestone both in its plan and in its architectural details (but Wivenhoe has the canopy set lower, has a less elaborate upper string course, and has no tile-hanging in the eastern gable). The Station Master's house section is very similar to that at Shenfield (demolished) also built 1886. It was restored in the late 1990s after getting into a poor state (and shows how attractive the station buildings on the Southend line could be if an effort were made). The flat-roofed section which might be taken for an extension is almost certainly original as it is already present on the 1896 OS. The little canopy above the house door is to the same design as those on staff cottages (Chapter 6).

Althorne and Fambridge on the New Essex lines in 1889 (both demolished), and Trimley (Suffolk) in 1890, had main buildings to the same design as Wivenhoe, but had detached Station Master's houses.

top
Frinton station was provided for the nascent upmarket residential resort in 1888 and conveys an appropriate sense of homely superiority. The contract went to F. Dupont in May 1887. The 'striped gable' had appeared at Waltham Cross (demolished) in 1885 and was about to feature at the New Essex lines stations, but Frinton differs from the others in that the gable starts at eaves level and there is a separate canopy above the doorway. The circular windows are so far as is known unique to Frinton. When compared with Wivenhoe, Frinton lacks the upper string course and the 'keystones' for the principal windows. The end gables are tile-hung.

middle
Detail of the Wivenhoe canopy, which employs the double struts that were repeated soon afterwards at the New Essex lines stations.

bottom right
The canopy at Frinton.

bottom left
Wivenhoe window.

The standard features of the New Essex lines architecture are seen in this late GER view of Rayleigh. The signal boxes went in the 1930s, and the original canopy valancing at all these stations was removed in the 1950s for electrification. The footbridges have all lost their roofs and been disfigured by high corrugated fencing.

The Southend line stations were built by Bennett Bros of Downham Market as subcontractors to Walter Scott & Co. the principal contractor for the line.

The Lens of Sutton Collection

Rayleigh (seen here) and Burnham on Crouch represent one of the standard arrangements for the larger New Essex lines stations, having an integral Station Master's house at one end, and a Booking Office pavilion half way along the main single-storey range, with half-hip roof forming a canopy above the main doorway. (As already noted, the half-hip roof with striped gable had appeared earlier at Waltham Cross in 1885). The Station Master's house has a rough-cast upper storey (as contemporary staff cottages – p.51) and tile-hung gables. The end gable at the left hand end of the main range is also tile-hung. On both the road and platform sides the openings are flat-arched, except for the Booking Hall doorways and two windows in the ground floor of the house, which are segmental-arched.

A copy of the original elevations and plans survives. It is dated 13th April 1886 – most design work was of course done 1-3 years before opening – and headed 'BURNHAM STATION' with a subsequent handwritten addition 'This design applies also to Rayleigh station'. The drawings are as the two stations were built, except that some diagonal timbers are shown in the gables, and some canopy ironwork details differ.

Rayleigh remains intact, but Burnham, which is 'handed' the same way, lost the Booking Office pavilion and everything to the left of it in 1968.

top

At Wickford the main building was in the same Domestic Revival style as subsequent stations further down the line, but to a one-off plan. The Booking Office 'pavilion' protrudes forward much further from the main range, as seen here, and its canopy has single struts not double. Wickford has also been altered much more than the other stations, losing all the original up side range in the 1970s, and the upper parts of the Station Master's house in 1998 after a fire. The Booking Office was enlarged and the new entrance added in 1981. (For the platform canopies at Billericay and Wickford see p.45).

middle

A second common arrangement for larger stations was found at Rochford (seen here in 2001) and Southminster. The Station Master's house features a very large striped gable on the road side, but is hipped on the platform side; again it is roughcast on the upper floor. There is one tile-hung gable on the end. The Booking Office pavilion has a large striped gable and no canopy. Here all the windows on the ground floor of the house are segmental-arched, as again are the Booking Hall doorways.

At both Rayleigh and Rochford the original road side doorway in the pavilion became a window in the electrification period improvements, with new entrances made to the right of the pavilion.

bottom right

Southminster in 1983. It is handed the opposite way to Rochford. As at Burnham, the Booking Office pavilion and everything to the left was demolished in 1968.

The building has recently been restored, but with incorrect windows.

bottom left

Canopy struts, Rayleigh.

top

At Hockley (seen here) and Prittlewell, and at the now-demolished Battlesbridge and Cold Norton, the Station Masters' houses were detached, the station building consisting simply of a single-storey gabled range with central Booking Office pavilion in the Rayleigh / Burnham style. Again all the windows on the road side were flat-arched but the Booking Hall doorway (now a window) was segmental-arched. The end gables were tile-hung. The pavilion gable is striped at Hockley but tile-hung at Prittlewell.

At Battlesbridge the detached Station Master's house survives (p.53), the others are demolished.

This view also shows (right) the hipped-roof Goods Lock-Up provided at stations which had no Goods Shed.

second left

A closer view of the road side canopy at Hockley. The wooden struts are carved in a different way at each station.

third left

A corresponding view of Prittlewell, where, in addition to the tile-hanging, the dimensions of the gable and canopy are different.

bottom left

Southend Victoria (1889) is an assembly of hipped and plain-gabled single-storey buildings of different heights, all in red brick with ashlar dressings. Unfortunately the intrusive new roads and concrete footbridge now make the station difficult to appreciate. This is the west side range where two striped gables (the other is on the north end, invisible here) provide the only direct link with the other stations on the line. There was originally a timber porte-cochere on this side.

After Norwich Thorpe, Ashbee's next major station rebuilding had been Hertford East (1888), also 'Free Renaissance' but more Dutch / mild Jacobean in its details. Southend provides the next variation on the major terminus theme, adding in a touch of Ashbee Domestic Revival.

bottom right

Gateway at Southend Victoria.

Several four-centred archways and doorways are featured at Southend – this pair form the main south frontage entrance.

Window details at Southend. These windows are very similar to some at Hertford East.

Buckhurst Hill was largely rebuilt in 1891/2, the only survivals from the previous buildings being the 1856 station house and an 1881/2 block of waiting rooms with canopy at the south end of the up platform (p.43). The rebuilding contract was given to T.Bennett in June 1891 for the large sum of £5,162. The line is in cutting here and the road level entrance building is actually a two-storey structure. This GER period view shows the dainty triple iron and glass canopy, long since removed. The general design of the building is similar to the 1887 street level building at Billericay (another station in a cutting) which still exists but greatly defaced. The segmental arches of the large windows and the doorway are of red brick alternating with ashlar; everything else is in red brick.

CHAPPEL

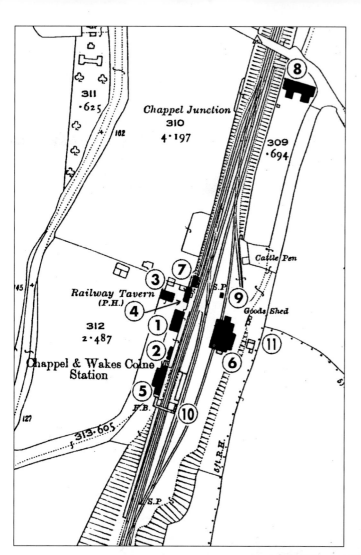

Ordnance Survey 25in map, 1920 survey. Railway buildings extant in 2005 shaded in black.

1. Original EUR station house, c1850, with single-storey extensions at rear of c1880-90.

2. 1850s-80s platform buildings, two-storey, built into embankment.

3. 'Sunderland Arms' alias 'Railway Tavern'.

4. Station coal shed, originally stables until 1891 (c1860s, now derelict).

5. 1891 station buildings and platform canopies (up platform building and canopy removed 1960s).

6. 1891 Goods Shed.

7. 1892 Signal Box.

8. 1891 Staff Cottages.

9. Traffic Office.

Buildings demolished –

10. 1891 footbridge (demolished 1960s).
11. 1891 Stables.

Buildings etc re-erected by East Anglian Railway Museum since the 1970s (not shown on map) -

Mistley Signal Box ('Chappel North') – see p.68.
Fotherby (GNR) Signal Box ('Chappel South').
1887 footbridge from Sudbury re-erected at Chappel 1981 on site of 1891 footbridge - see p.48.
Smith's Bookstall from North Harrow (1936), in Booking Hall.
Crane from Saffron Walden (in Goods Shed).
Cast-iron Urinal from Cockfield.

---

middle When the Sudbury line opened in 1849 there was no station at Chappel, but there had been plans for one from the start and it was soon provided at an unknown date c1850. Money was very short at this date so it is no surprise that only a simple station house was provided – a great come-down from the EUR's glorious days of 1846/7! The single-storey extensions at the rear were added c1880-90. Now known as the 'Old Station House'.

bottom left The old platform buildings seem to be of three periods. The left hand section (ending just to the right of the door) is probably of c1850 given that it is built in the same unusual two-headers-and-one-stretcher bond as the Station House. The remainder of the sloping-roof section, in English bond, is 1860s-70s, and the flat-roofed section at right probably 1880s (it had a water tank on the roof, removed c1975). In later years the rooms at platform level served as Porters' Room (north end) and Lamp Room (south end, under tank).

bottom right The Sunderland Arms, renamed the Railway Tavern c1890, was built around 1860/61 in hopes of capitalising on the station's new junction status. Its first landlords Joseph Appleby and Henry Palmer also doubled as the station coal merchants.

The original single-platform Chappel station was far from ideal after the Colne Valley line opened in 1861, but things remained unaltered until 1891, when Chappel was made a two-platform passing place with generous new station buildings and a large new goods shed. The building contract was given to Alfred Coe of Ipswich in November 1890 at £2,990. The main station building was a two-storey edifice in bright red brick, owing to the platform being on embankment. The platform-level Booking Hall was accessed via a double external stairway which was originally covered by a valanced canopy. This was removed in the 1960s, leaving unfortunate scars; otherwise there have been no significant external changes to the buildings. The flat-roofed section at left was the Gents.

In the March 1891 drawings for the new station the windows are all shown as significantly segmental-arched, but were almost flat-arched as built.

The much smaller new station building at Harringay Park (1894) was built with many of the same details as Chappel.

For some reason the platform canopies at Chappel were not to the standard pattern; instead they have these large and elaborate 'double wheel' brackets (also found at Snaresbrook, c1894), and the valancing is a simplified version of the standard type with alternate concave and convex cut boards. Sixteen of these brackets were ordered for the new station.

The Chappel station buildings retain two of the 'GER' fireplaces that were installed at many new stations in the 1880s and 1890s. There is another, slightly different in design, in the goods shed office.

In the Booking Hall at Chappel is the Colne Valley & Halstead Railway's 1914-18 war memorial, originally in the Booking Hall at Halstead.

above left

The 1891 Chappel goods shed probably takes pride of place among the county's surviving goods sheds, remaining in largely original condition both externally and internally. (The only major alteration is that a window at the north end has been converted to a door by the EARM to give ramped access). The plinth is in engineering brick and the remainder of the building in red brick. All the windows are semicircular-arched with radial glazing. The goods shed at Docking (Norfolk) was similar. The loading bay canopy has the same valancing as the station platform canopies.

above right

The goods yard crane at Chappel (a rare survival) was made by the Kirkstall Forge Co. in 1865. We may guess that it came here in 1891 second-hand from one of the stations on the '1865' lines. Inside the goods shed is another crane which was obtained by the EARM from Saffron Walden.

bottom left

To the north of the goods shed is this 'Traffic Office' where a clerk laboured on behalf of the Railway Clearing House, his presence being required because of inter-company transfers between the GER and the CV&HR. It was built some time between 1876 and 1896.

bottom right

Not strictly part of Essex's railway heritage, this splendid cast iron urinal was brought from Cockfield (Suffolk) by the EARM.

Chappel signal box was built in 1891/2 and opened in May 1892, provided by the signalling contractors Saxby & Farmer as part of the full resignalling required for the new layout. It is to the design now known as 'GER Type 7', which was the most common signal box type in Essex. The lever frame (which had to be reinstalled by the EARM after being thrown out by BR) is a 38-lever Saxby & Farmer 1888 Patent Duplex. This box has been restored but has no working function. At left is the original stables building.

The terrace of four red brick staff cottages at Chappel were also built in 1891, replacing an earlier terrace of four nearby. Alfred Coe had this as a separate contract, let in November 1890 at £958 4s 5d. It was specified that 'the first two shall be completed on or before the 11th day of January 1891, the second two on or before the first day of April 1891'. These cottages are to the same design as the terrace of six built at Prittlewell in 1892. The doors have an unusual arrangement of lintel plus segmental relieving arch above, without the usual small canopy.

A large new down side building had been provided at Colchester in 1865 and formed the principal entrance to the station in the years thereafter. The up side facilities remained primitive, even though most passengers were for London trains. In April 1892 a Colchester Corporation deputation visited the GER Board and was told that work could begin on new up side buildings 'later this year'. On 4th October 1892 the Board approved plans, estimated at £31,500. However money was tight at this time and the contract for the main buildings was not actually let until October 1894, A.J.Bateman of Ramsey (Hunts) getting the job for £8,725. The work was reported complete in November 1896. The main building is still in good original condition today, save for some modern doorways/windows having been inserted on the ground floor. Unfortunately it is all but invisible to station users! The 300ft-long range is to a symmetrical plan. It forms a further variation in Ashbee's major station theme, this time with Baroque / classical details. The two-storey central pavilion has a hipped roof and Baroque pediment, and there are further single-storey hipped roof pavilions at each end of the range. Construction is in red brick with ashlar dressings. There were also extensive wide platform canopies behind, but these were all dismantled c1960, leaving the plainer rear elevation of the building exposed in a manner not intended.

BRITISH RAILWAYS

top right
  Detail of the pediment.

bottom right
  Detail of window in the western pavilion. These windows are different from the windows in the eastern pavilion.

top left
  The cupola/vent and the little lantern turrets. Hertford East had a cupola/vent of this type, as did Ilford (1893, demolished).

second left
  Detail of the eastern pavilion. Both pavilions have Ionic capitals.

third left
  The canopy which stretches for most of the length of the road side has non-standard columns and brackets (although the brackets are similar in spirit to the standard type). The semicircular-arched windows have brick and ashlar arches reminiscent of Buckhurst Hill.

above

Following a 'complaint from Col. M.C. Browning', the GER Board authorised the preparation of plans for a new station at Manningtree in August 1892, but it was only in May 1897 that the project was given the go-ahead. Most of the work was done in 1899-1900, with completion in 1901. The new main range on the up side was long and low, with only the one cross-gable above the main entrance to break the skyline. Construction is in red brick with ash-lar dressings including a string course level with the bottom of the windows. All the windows are segmental-arched. There is a smaller building on the down side. Both platforms had extensive 'standard' canopies, but the down plat-form canopy and the east end of the up platform canopy have been removed. The goods facilities were also rebuilt; the goods shed is demolished but the stables survive (p.66).

right

Several examples of the original window glass survive at Manningtree – this is the down side General Waiting Room.

The rebuilding of Witham station was agreed to in February 1905 after a visit by the GER Way & Works Committee mem-bers. The contract was given to S.A.Kenney in October 1906 at £6,735, and the work was completed in spring 1908. Witham is actually one of the most intact remaining GER-built stations, however its location in a cutting prevents it from being visually impressive, and the road-level entrance seen here is just a front wall, though pleasant enough. The Booking Office behind the front wall is supported on girders over the track.

This timber-built block on the up platform at Elsenham was provided in 1902, the contract going to J.Glassock in September 1901 at £530. The canopy is fully 'stan-dard'. A couple of feet had to be shaved off the width for electrification in the 1980s. (Photograph 1982).

The last significant station building erected by the GER in present-day Essex was the up side Booking Office at Elsenham. It was probably erected in 1913 in con-junction with the opening of the Thaxted branch. The lower courses are in engi-neering bricks and the rest in red brick. (Photograph 1982).

CHAPTER FIVE

GREAT EASTERN RAILWAY PLATFORM CANOPIES AND STATION FOOTBRIDGES

PLATFORM CANOPIES

In the early decades, lengthy full-width platform canopies were hardly known. Stations where cover was deemed appropriate had overall 'trainshed' roofs. Otherwise there might be just a narrow verandah in front of the main building itself (as at Audley End or Great Chesterford) or a smaller open-fronted covered waiting area (as at the Harwich line and Tendring Hundred stations); plus a small waiting shelter on the 'other' platform. Many stations had no platform cover at all, and for many passengers Waiting Rooms were of great importance, the platform only being ventured onto as the train arrived.

Trainshed roofs went out of fashion, except for the very largest stations, after the 1850s, and platform canopies appeared in lieu at town and suburban stations. To give a GER example, all the stations on Edward Wilson's Bethnal Green – Edmonton / Walthamstow lines (opened 1870-73) had lengthy canopies, of the ridge-and-furrow type, with sawtooth valancing. Walthamstow Central and Edmonton Green are the best surviving examples. Such ridge-and-furrow canopies appeared elsewhere on the GER up to 1885, the 1883 down platform at Ipswich being one of the last; but no station in present-day Essex had them. Indeed, we cannot really go into the question of 1860s/70s GER canopies here, as very little survives in Essex from this period.

By the late 1870s both Edward Wilson & Co., and the GER's own Engineer's department, had largely changed instead to flat-roofed canopies (which actually have a slight slope for rainwater purposes). John Wilson and Neville Ashbee evolved the soon-to-become-'standard' GER canopy valancing, in a MkI version in three-board units at Seven Sisters and West Green (1878) and on the Wroxham – County School line (1879-82), and then in a MkII version in five-board units, first found on the Mildenhall branch opened in 1884/5. (See photos at p.44 top). However, the GER engineers under Langley stuck to saw-tooth valancing until 1883/4. Then, when Wilson and Ashbee moved to the GER staff, they were able to make their 'standard' valancing near-universal. But several different designs of columns and brackets were still used in the mid-1880s, and it was only from 1888/9 that a fuller standardisation of column, bracket, and valancing was imposed for most new work.

Early canopies, including some of the GER's earliest flat canopies, were often of all-timber construction, with timber columns and diagonal timber struts. By the late 1870s cast-iron columns and brackets (alias 'spandrels') were more common. By the time of standardisation c1888 the GER was also regularly incorporating longitudinal girders between the columns, for extra rigidity, although the roofing was still carried on transverse timber beams. Eventually, by 1900, some of the larger new canopies were given transverse girders as well.

Canopies can from another angle be categorised into three types depending on locational details, (1) those which are supported entirely on large brackets fixed to the station buildings or other walls, (2) those which rest on the station building or other walls on the inside, and on a line of columns on the outside, and (3) those on island platforms which are supported on two lines of columns (latterly sometimes on a single line of centrally-placed columns only). In the early years columns were often placed dangerously close to the platform edge.

Almost all GER stations built from the mid-1880s on had extensive platform canopies. Many earlier stations had canopies added in the 1870s-90s, e.g. Braintree and Dovercourt. Unfortunately, the majority of canopies have been reduced in length or removed altogether since the 1960s. Many in Essex have also had their valancing removed in connection with overhead electrification.

page 42 top

Most GER canopies up to c1885 had sawtooth valancing, usually curved sawtooth as seen here at Dovercourt (1882), but sometimes straight. Details varied – some had small holes (or larger trefoil-shaped holes) in the middle of each board, some holes between the boards, etc.

This type of bracket with the quatrefoil in a circle feature was the most common type for work on existing lines c1878-82 (but is not found on E.Wilson & Co. new lines).

The canopy columns at Dovercourt are plain and round-section, on an octagonal-section base, with plain round-section capitals. Buckhurst Hill and Brentwood have the same type of column.

above left

The 1882 up island Waiting Rooms block canopy at Thorpe-le-Soken, showing the 'GER in quatrefoil, plus mouchettes' type brackets that were the most common type for work on existing lines c1882-4 (again, not found on the new lines). This type of bracket is not to be confused with the perhaps better-known but quite different 'GER' brackets found at the 1903 Fairlop Loop stations.

Other Essex stations still having this type of bracket are Buckhurst Hill up side (1881/2), Brentwood down side (1884), Theydon Bois (1884), and St Botolph's (1884).

Whilst many of the brackets and other ironwork used by the railway companies were stock items taken from the catalogues of the country's leading ironworks, others such as these were clearly produced specially.

above right

The 1881/2 Buckhurst Hill up platform Waiting Rooms block.

below

St Botolph's (Colchester Town), showing the canopy erected along the front of the 1866 main building in 1884, as part of the improvements effected here after the GER took over the Tendring Hundred Railway. The 'GER' brackets here are more finely cast than those at Thorpe-le-Soken. The valancing is straight sawtooth with holes between the boards. This 'flat' canopy has a very noticeable fall to the front, created by the insertion of wedge-shaped pieces of timber between the brackets and the transverse beams.

page 42 bottom

The down platform canopy at Bishops Stortford (date not known, but post-1879) has brackets to the same design as Dovercourt but it will be noted that they are more thickly-cast in this case. As with most earlier canopies, there are no longitudinal members between the columns here – the columns just support transverse timber beams into which the main longitudinal roofing timbers are set as seen here. The round-section columns have foliage-decorated capitals, as on many 1870s GER canopies, although the detail of the decoration varies. The canopy was cut back in width and the original valancing removed in the pre-electrification works.

The up island platform canopy at Bishops Stortford is to virtually the same design, but this is partly a coincidence as it was (re-)erected in 1927, using components from the 1885-built Newmarket Old Station High Level island platform canopy, after the original canopy had been largely demolished in a train collision during the 1926 General Strike.

left middle

Ingatestone (1885), Newport (c1885), and Wivenhoe (1886) have identical canopies, featuring MkII 'standard' valancing, and brackets to the design shown in this photograph of Newport.

The 1890 up side Waiting Room block canopy at Great Bentley also has these brackets.

bottom left

Part of the up platform canopy at Newport is supported solely on the side of the platform buildings and has larger brackets to this more elaborate design. For more general views of the Newport canopies see p.25.

right middle

The columns at these three stations (photo shows Wivenhoe) are round-section with an octagonal base. There are two rings immediately above the base, the upper one knobbed; and two rings further up with Tudor roses between them. The capitals (seen in previous view of Newport) are square-section.

page 44 top left

The 'MkI' version of the GER 'standard' valancing was developed around 1878. This version did not appear in Essex, except for an extra-elaborate one at Parkeston Quay (1883, see p.54 - canopy now demolished). The photograph here shows one of the stations on the Wroxham - County School line.

In this MkI version the pattern is formed by groups of three boards, two of which are mirror-images forming an ogee-curve downpoint, and the third having a concave cut-out. (There is however an aberration at one point in the canopy illustrated here).

page 44 top right

The MkII 'standard' valancing, first seen at the 1882-designed and 1884-built Mildenhall branch stations. This is a view of the Maldon East canopy of 1891.

The pattern in this type is formed by groups of five boards, with two concave-cut and one convex-cut boards between each pair of ogee downpoint boards. In most examples (as here) there were holes between every fifth board, however there were also many canopies with no holes.

This type of valancing became one of the enduring symbols of the GER network, remaining 'current' until the end of station building c1913, and therefore extremely widespread.

this page right

The most elaborate surviving ironwork at any Essex station is found in the 1886 canopy at Braintree. The brackets are a development of those used at the Mildenhall branch stations in 1884/5, which featured the main roundel only; and those in the 1880s ridge and furrow canopies at Ipswich and March. The columns are of quatrefoil section. The MkII standard valancing here has unusually large holes.

below

The 1887-built canopies at Billericay (seen here) and Wickford introduced the use of longitudinal girders between the columns. This required four brackets per column. The two transverse brackets are of the Ingatestone/Newport/Wivenhoe type, the lower longitudinal brackets are of a new quarter-circle design. (In GER canopies, the longitudinal members are always set below the transverse members). The columns at Billericay and Wickford are of the Ingatestone/Newport/Wivenhoe type except for having a completely different design of capital as seen here. These two stations had MkII standard valancing, now removed.

Interestingly, the 1886 drawings for Burnham / Rayleigh show columns and brackets of this type, another case (like Newport) of the canopy details being 'updated' to the latest design at the time of construction even though the main building was still built as per the drawings.

top left

The new 'standard' column and bracket designs introduced in 1888 completed the process of canopy standardisation, which was made conspicuous by the use of the new design for all stations beyond Wickford on the New Essex lines.

A few early examples of the new standard canopies had no longitudinal girders and therefore had transverse brackets only, as seen here at Stansted (1890). Stansted also has transverse brackets on one side only, probably because of the narrow width.

'Standard' columns are of round section with octagonal bases. They have four short lengths of fluting in the main portion of the column.

top right

All the stations on the new lines beyond Wickford, however, had longitudinal girders, which then became the norm. This view of Burnham-on-Crouch shows the new designs of transverse bracket and quarter-circle longitudinal bracket.

Burnham-on-Crouch and Southminster have reduced-length canopies but still have their MkII standard valancing. Rayleigh, Hockley, Rochford and Prittlewell retain their full-length canopies but the valancing was removed for electrification.

middle

A general view of the Prittlewell down platform canopy roofing. At these stations the transverse beams rest at the rear on timber corbels in the walling.

bottom

The 1894 down platform Waiting Rooms block at Audley End has a canopied area with longitudinal girders and quarter-circle longitudinal brackets. The building is in yellow brick with red brick segmental arches above the doorways.

46

top left

Later 'standard' canopies had a much less exciting type of small solid bracket (actually part of the main column casting) for the longitudinal girders, as seen here at Witham. Chelmsford and Manningtree are also of this type.

top right

Sections of 'standard' canopy supported on station buildings often had these large circle type brackets. They are of considerable length, stretching down to platform level. Photograph shows Witham.

bottom right

Standardisation was never universal - Special designs of canopy were used for the main line quadruplings in London, and the Fairlop Loop. The largest stations also necessarily had more elaborate canopies. This 1930s view shows the 1889 Southend Victoria platform canopies (which are no longer conveniently photographed due to new roof cladding). Columns of this design were used by the GER for a number of 'superior' stations in the late 1880s-1914 period.

bottom left

Non-standard brackets were also still used after the late 1880s for a few locations, e.g. Chappel (p.37) and here on the road side canopy of the new Bishops Stortford up side Booking Office of 1899.

STATION FOOTBRIDGES

Many Essex station footbridges have been replaced since the 1950s by new concrete or steel footbridges with higher headroom for overhead electrification, and only fifteen pre-1920s footbridges now remain in the county. All are in fact of 1880s or 1890s vintage, a period when many stations that previously had only flat crossings between the platforms were given footbridges. All fifteen are of cast-/wrought-iron construction.

top right
1880s GER footbridges were mostly of plain plate-sided construction. This is the present footbridge at Chappel which was originally at Sudbury (1887) and was re-erected here in 1981. Most station footbridges were originally covered, but many had their coverings removed in the early 20th century when local authorities insisted on charging higher rates for covered bridges.

second right
The other two remaining plate-sided bridges are Ingatestone and Wivenhoe, which were built by the Cleveland Bridge & Engineering Co., under a single contract given on 16th February 1886. This is Ingatestone, which was raised prior to electrification. The south side is supported on cast iron columns but the north side has brick steps; some of the new 1950s brickwork for the raising can be seen. (See *Great Eastern Journal* 87.4 for an earlier view). The original purpose of the elegantly-built 1850s brick hut at left is not known for certain.
Wivenhoe was also raised for electrification, but subsequently the original span was replaced by a new higher span.

left
The lattice trussed girder footbridge at Theydon Bois (1885) is an example of a type that was not only a 'standard' on the GER in the late 1880s, but also appeared in virtually identical form on several other companies' lines (including the LT&SR, but none survive there).
Whilst the major national ironworks were regularly supplying bridgework to many different railway companies, it was normally the practice for the railway company to specify all design details, and the 'link' in this case is not yet understood.

left
Several footbridges retain their original maker's plates. The Theydon Bois bridge was part of a contract given to Arrols on 16th December 1884 for two bridges at £215 each. The other was for Fordham and photographs of it can be seen in Peter Paye's Mildenhall Branch book.
Arrols at this time were building both the Tay Bridge and the Forth Bridge, the greatest engineering works of the day - but ordinary jobs continued notwithstanding!

top

The stations from Wickford to Prittlewell inclusive all had lattice footbridges of the Theydon Bois type, and all five still exist. However they are considerably altered; all were lifted prior to electrification on to new high concrete bases, in addition to which a section of steel girder was inserted above the capitals (as seen here at Wickford) for further height gain. However the main purpose of this view is to show the quatrefoil decoration in the castings of this footbridge type.

middle

Epping (1892) represents a lattice type of c1890 (of which Alresford and Great Bentley also survive, but with replacement spans). Here the main span is straight and in consequence the staircases are longer and have a landing halfway up. The columns are very plain, without the fluted section seen on the Theydon Bois type.

bottom left

Debden (1891) represents the last GER standard footbridge type, used from c1890 into the 1900s. We have a partly-curved lattice span again, and plain columns as at Epping. The present footbridge roofing is a London Transport replacement (the original roof having been removed at an earlier date).

bottom right

One of the maker's plates at Debden – the other is dated 1890!

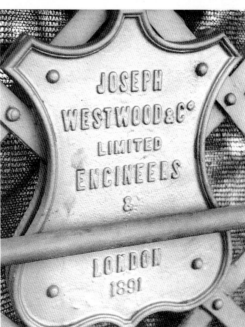

49

CHAPTER SIX

GREAT EASTERN RAILWAY STAFF HOUSING
with a feature on Parkeston

Railway companies built many staff cottages, both in towns and in rural areas, if insufficient existing accommodation was available in the area, or if duties required a man to live close by a station. The GER already had a fair number of inherited cottages in the 1860s (relatively few in Essex, though), but it was in the 1885 - 1914 period that most were built. In 1880 the GER Board decided that all new or rebuilt stations should include at least two cottages for staff. In 1892 it was reported that there were 1,281 cottages over its network as a whole, but more were still needed in rural areas. Accordingly it was agreed to allocate £30,000 per year for building cottages – this would buy about 120 cottages – until such time as a further 800 had been completed. This however did not come to pass, as rent levels started to become uneconomic in relation to construction costs. In 1900 it was noted that only 86 cottages had been built since 1892, and the idea of a major ongoing programme was abandoned. Nevertheless plenty of cottages were built in the 1900s, mostly of a cheaper type. A 1921 national survey showed the GER as having 1,322 staff dwellings excluding station houses (possibly calculated on a different basis to the 1892 figure?). This actually gave the GER only 18th position out of the 23 larger companies surveyed in number of houses / number of employees terms.

Only an introduction to GER cottages can be given here, restricted to the types surviving in Essex. A definitive account of the various standard types must await further study across the whole GER network.

Some 200 GER cottages remain in Essex; unfortunately almost all have been disfigured over the last twenty years by new windows and other 'improvements' and extensions destroying their character.

Station Masters' Houses have already been dealt with in Chapters 1-4 where forming part of the main station buildings; at other locations a separate house was provided for the Station Master, and one such is illustrated here.

Crossing Houses were provided at most level crossings in the earlier decades of the railway system; in many cases the Act of Incorporation required the company to build a 'lodge' at all public road crossings, for a resident keeper to attend to the gates. The three views at p. 53 show surviving Essex examples from the 1840s. For later examples see Easton Lodge (p.24) and Frinton (p.20).

left middle
This pair of cottages at Hatfield Peverel were authorised in 1876 for the signalmen, before the station existed; but the contract was not actually let until April 1880. They cost £498. They are built in yellow brick with two three-course bands of bright red brick at mid-window level on each floor. The windows are modern.

bottom
The Ashbee Domestic Revival style had taken hold by the time larger-scale GER cottage building began. This is part of a terrace of six built at Clacton in 1885, in red brick, with the two end houses as gabled 'pavilions' with tile-hung gables. W.T.Hook had the contract at £1,080. Canopies of this type above the front doors were to feature on most GER houses until the 1900s. They must be highly regarded by owners as they normally seem to survive however many other 'improvements' are carried out! All the windows seen here are modern renewals.

There are two terraces to this exact design, and another two very similar, at Parkeston (p.56).

right middle
These cottages next to the line in Chigwell Lane, Debden, were built in 1896, and another terrace of four at Ongar built in 1892 to this design also survive.

A different terrace design of this period, of which examples exist at Prittlewell and Chappel, is illustrated at p.39.

The most familiar GER cottage type in Essex are the red-brick pairs with half-hip roofs built c1885-c1905. The earliest known examples, two pairs at Shenfield c1886 (one of which is seen here) and one pair at Wrabness in 1886 (now badly altered), had a wholly-brick frontage. Three further pairs were provided at Shenfield in 1901/2 to match.

In an amended version with tile-hung gables and the upper floor roughcast, the design was reproduced liberally on the New Essex lines in 1888/9. The window heads are also arranged differently.

The surviving examples on these lines are
One pair at Ramsden Bellhouse (Church Road)
One pair at Hawkwell (off Rectory Road)
One pair at Rochford
Two pairs at Prittlewell
Three pairs at Woodham Ferrers
One pair at Hogwell
Three pairs at Fambridge
Two pairs at Althorne
Two pairs at Southminster
Two pairs at Maldon West
This is the Rochford pair, which still retain the original style windows with three horizontal glazing bars, as used in most GER cottage designs.

below

One of the Maldon West pairs (1889), showing also the lengthy boundary wall in GER Engineer's brick that remains in situ here. GR 842063.

top

A design of rather different spirit was used for two semi-detached pairs at Ingatestone in 1903, situated in Stock Lane next to the 1557 Almshouses (GR 653996). They are in a pale white brick, with bands of bright red brick. But for the game being given away by the canopies one would hardly recognise them as GER-built. The small-pane windows are original.

Many of the GER cottage building contracts survive at the Public Record Office, and in this case, unusually, a drawing is attached. It is titled 'GER Standard Workmen's Cottage, in pairs or any other number'. They have a Living Room, Kitchen, and Scullery downstairs, and three bedrooms upstairs. To date no other cottages have been found to this design.

middle

These two pairs of red brick gabled-roof cottages were provided at Manningtree (GR 096322) in 1905 (there is also a pair to this design at Nos 11 and 12 Alexander Lane, Shenfield, also 1905). The usual segmental-arched windows appear, but the ground floor windows and doors unusually have 'keystones'. In this 2001 view the right hand cottage still had its original windows, sadly since replaced. These four cottages were built by A.Coe for £888 (compared to £1,033 for the four at Ingatestone).

bottom

Most later GER cottages were in cheaper gabled terraces. This terrace of four in yellow brick at Rochford dates from 1912. The same design was used for a total of 45 cottages in Essex in 1912-15, the others (which all survive) being

Ongar (2-14 Bansons Lane)   terrace of seven, 1912

Tolleshunt D'Arcy   single cottage, 1912   (much altered)

Braintree one pair, 1912

52

Chelmsford (104-122 Arbour Lane) terrace of ten, 1912
Parkeston, Foster Rd north side   two terraces of ten, 1913 (photo p.57)
Shenfield (10 Alexander Lane) single cottage, 1915
  The windows and the upper floor roughcasting are as previous designs, but the door canopies are of a different type. The brickwork is corbelled out at the party walls. These cottages are of rectangular plan, with a lesser floor area than the earlier designs, which had back extensions.

below
  Ickleton Road level crossing at Great Chesterford (GR 502427) has a single-storey ECR crossing house of 1845, which is very much in the 18th/early 19th century country estate gate lodge style. It was probably designed by Sancton Wood / Thompson.

above
  At Ingatestone the small single-storey crossing house was built in the same style as the 1846 station building, with diapered brickwork.

below
  The fine Station Master's house at Battlesbridge (1889); there is another to this design at Althorne. The pargeting is recent!

above
  Mount Bures crossing house has much in common architecturally with the now-demolished Bures station building, and can therefore be assumed to date from the opening of the line in 1849. It is now empty.

below
  The only remaining manned level crossing in Essex with a house is Burrs Road, Clacton (GR 190175). The house was built by the LNER c1930 to replace the 1882 crossing house prior to widening of the line.

PARKESTON

The improvements carried out at Harwich in 1864-6 quickly proved insufficient for the GER's increasing continental traffic, and as early as 1874 an Act was obtained authorising the construction of a new 1800ft long quay on the mudflats west of Harwich. The work was done in 1879-83, with J.S.Macintyre and John Wilson as the Engineers. The new quay was generally referred to as 'the Stour Quay' initially, but in October 1881 the GER Board resolved to name it 'Parkeston Quay' in honour of their Chairman C.H.Parkes who was the leading force behind the company's expansion at this period. The new loop line opened in 1882, and the quay and passenger station on 15th March 1883. The 1883 quay frontage remains today, but there were big westward extensions in 1905-7 and 1931-4. The only pre-1960s building surviving today is the main 1883 'Parkeston Quay Hotel' block, which had the station offices incorporated in the ground floor. It has served as port offices since 1965.

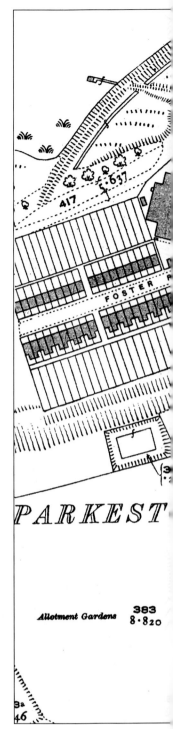

above
A GER period view of the Parkeston Quay Hotel. It was built by Bennett Bros as part of a £47,846 contract granted in February 1882, and had to be entirely supported on piles of 40 to 50ft in length. The architect is not certain. The whole building is in bright red brick, with ashlar dressings. This view also shows the original platform canopies (now removed) which were a more elaborate version of the MkI 'standard' canopy.
The Lens of Sutton Collection

left
A closer view of the Hotel's 'French' clock tower. The upper portion was removed in 1961.

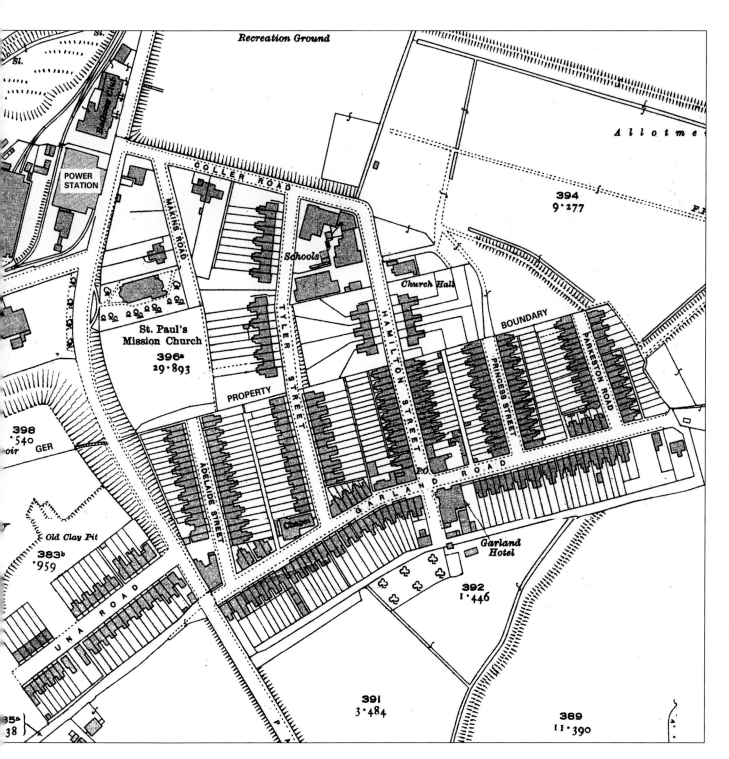

Ordnance Survey 25in map, 1922 survey

In December 1881 the GER Directors visited Harwich to discuss 'cottages for labourers' near the new quay, and at the time of the opening of the quay in 1883 it was announced that 'the company have acquired a large quantity of land and are preparing to build houses for the workforce, so that Parkeston is likely to become an important town in the course of a few years'. (Note the 'Parkeston' name already being used for the new settlement).

It might have seemed then that a planned 'railway' town was about to spring up, but things did not quite turn out so, or not immediately. The GER did eventually build a total of 77 houses, but the 'planning' was decidedly muddled.

For some reason the GER did next to nothing in the first years after 1883, and the original Parkeston settlement built mostly in 1883-5 was a private developers' speculation. It comprised closely-packed terraced housing in Adelaide St, Tyler St (south end), Hamilton St (south end), Princess St, Parkeston Rd, and along the north side of Garland Rd. These houses ran right up to the GER property boundary (it was impossible to build further south as the land was flood-prone). This non-GER housing was completed when the south side of Garland Rd was built up in the

1890s, followed by Una Rd in the 1900s, and finally by Edward St (not shown on this map) in the interwar years.

Building on GER land was much slower. £1,074 was authorised for 'Parkeston, cottages for staff' in August 1884; this was probably for the pair on the west side of Makins Rd (still there), and the pair on the south side of Coller Rd (demolished). The twenty cottages at the north end of Tyler St were provided in 1890, and the twelve at the north end of Hamilton St, with their peculiarly-shaped gardens, at an unknown date pre-1896. In 1899/1900 there followed the Enginemen's Barracks (alias Hamilton House) and twenty cottages on the south side of Foster Rd. The remaining twenty cottages on the north side of Foster Rd were built from 1913.

Coller Road, Makins Road, Tyler Street, Hamilton Street, and Foster Road were named after GER Directors. It is not clear whether the GER had laid down and/or named these streets at the start in 1883. Garland Road was named after the local landowner.

Public facilities in the non-GER section of Parkeston were the Wesleyan Chapel (1887) on the north side of Garland Rd, and the Garland Hotel (now renamed the 'Captain Fryatt'). There were two successive Anglican churches, both on GER land but not GER-built. The original St Gabriel's in Hamilton St (shown as 'Church

Hall' on this map, and now demolished) was replaced in 1914 by the larger St Paul's.

The school was built by the GER themselves in 1888. Initially the GER had paid in 1883 for the enlargement of the village school in Ramsey (in which parish Parkeston was situated), but the staff soon out-bred that! and in July 1886 the GER Board heard that there were 450 children in Parkeston but only 162 school places available for them. It was therefore decided to build a school under the company's own management, with the GER Directors serving as School Managers for legal purposes. However by the turn of the century this school was under local authority control. It was extended in 1902. The buildings remain but are no longer used as a school.

The 'Railway Club' at the top of the map extract was built in the early twentieth century but is no longer extant. Immediately south of it was the GER Power Station, built in 1895 and also now demolished. The large building to the west of the Power Station was a naval 'Torpedo Depot', rather oddly squeezed in here.

Parkeston has undergone little change since 1914. 74 of the 77 GER houses survive, as do most of the non-GER houses. However the attractive 'Recreation Ground' to the north of the housing area has now disappeared under vast acreages of lorry parking.

top left

Nos 1 and 2 Makins Rd, probably the first GER-built houses in Parkeston, do not appear to have been built to any GER design. There were a few cases elsewhere of the GER getting builders to construct ordinary style terraced houses for them.

top right

This is the terrace of six houses on the west side of Hamilton St. Given that they are to the same design as the 1885 Clacton terrace (p.50), we may surmise that they are of about that date, but no reference has been found in the minutes. The rendering here is a 20th-century alteration. As with almost all the ex-GER housing in Parkeston, there is now not one original window left.

middle

The two GER terraces on the west side of Tyler St. The contract for these was given to A.J.Bateman in May 1890. They differ from the Clacton /Hamilton St type in having more steeply pitched gables for the end houses, without the tile-hanging; also the middle eight have a lower eaves level with a single large first floor window each, instead of two small windows. The latter feature is shared with the Chappel and Prittlewell cottages built shortly afterwards (p.39).

bottom

The western of the two terraces (of ten cottages each) on the south side of Foster Road, which were built under a £10,467 contract given to H.J.Linzell in March 1899, which also included the Barracks. The frontal appearance of these houses is quite similar to the later houses on the north side of the road, but there is no upper floor rough-casting here, and there are no door canopies. As can be seen from the map, these are also bigger houses than those on the north side, slightly wider and with a back extension.

right

The cottages on the north side of Foster Road are the same as the 1912 Rochford cottages (p.52), to a rectangular plan. This is the western of the two terraces of ten, built 1913 or soon after. The canopies have mostly been converted to porches.

middle and bottom

The GER 'Enginemen's Barracks' at the east end of Foster Road were built to accommodate fifty men (men from other loco depots whose duties required them to spend the night here before returning home on another train the next day). The accommodation was quite luxurious by comparison with such facilities elsewhere! It was reported in February 1901 that the Barracks had opened.

However it is not really evident why the company considered such a large number of beds necessary here, and there was indeed no such great need in the event. The building had already been let off as a factory by 1913, and is now offices.

CHAPTER SEVEN

THE LONDON TILBURY & SOUTHEND RAILWAY

The railway system of South Essex was created by the London Tilbury & Southend Railway, which started life as an offshoot of the Eastern Counties but was an independent company by the 1860s. The LT&SR was not famed for the elegance of its station buildings, nor, thanks to the largely flat area traversed, did it possess many notable engineering features.

No LT&SR station buildings from the early decades survive. The earliest now extant in Essex is Shoeburyness (1884) which, unusually, was timber-built.

For the stations on its new lines opened 1885-1892 (Dagenham, 1885, demolished: Hornchurch, 1885, demolished: Upminster, 1885: West Horndon, 1886: Laindon, 1888: Pitsea, 1888, demolished: and Ockendon, 1892) the LT&SR adopted a fully standardised architectural policy for the first and only time. These lines were engineered by Arthur Stride the LT&SR Manager and Engineer, with James Robertson as Resident Engineer. However the station buildings were essentially copied from those built by George Hopkins on the Ely – Newmarket line (1879) and on the London Chatham & Dover Railway's Maidstone – Ashford line (1884). Stride had strong Kent connections, having been on the LC&DR

before joining the LT&SR in 1875, and we may guess that he saw the Maidstone – Ashford stations and liked the design.

In 1889 the LT&SR rebuilt its largest station, Southend (Central), to improve the facilities in response to the start of GER competition in the town. The new station was a single-storey red brick grouping with segmental-arched windows. It was enlarged in 1899 in the same style.

New stations at Westcliff (1895) and Leigh-on-Sea (1897) bought a change from red brick, to yellow brick with bright red brick dressings.

For its last two stations at Thorpe Bay (1910) and Benfleet (1911), the LT&SR belatedly turned to a weak Domestic Revival style, with striped gables and rough-casting of the upper floor. In many ways these were the company's most attractive stations. It would seem likely that James Robertson, who was formally appointed as LT&SR Engineer in 1899, designed the later stations, but no specific reference is known.

The LT&SR was taken over by the Midland Railway in 1912 but due to the onset of war that company did not carry out any new station works on the system.

Railway Station, Shoeburyness. 13.

A.H.Judd &Co
Southend-on-Sea

Shoeburyness suffered a serious fire in 1891 and there are no pre-fire photographs, so we cannot be sure that the 1884 appearance was exactly as later. It is not clear why this station was timber-built; other timber station buildings on the LT&SR were on marshland and thus necessarily so. It has all the air of an 1850s 'temporary' station.

The platform canopy seems to be original but has brackets of the Benfleet type (p.63) so perhaps these were added for strengthening c1910. The outer edge of the canopy was cut back to the pillars in the 1980s. Otherwise everything remains as in this Edwardian view.

This c1960 view of West Horndon shows the general arrangement of the LT&SR 1880s new lines station buildings. At one end is the two-storey Station Master's house, on an L plan, with gabled roofs and corbelled verges. The Booking Hall section at centre is single-storey with a hipped roof, entered by a protruding porch with canopy above. The valancing is of the same type as used on the platform canopies. At the opposite end to the house West Horndon and Upminster have a sizeable pavilion with corbelling as seen here, but Laindon and Ockendon have only a smaller and lower plain-gabled block.

above left
Roadside view of Laindon from the house end. The Booking Office section (right) was enlarged c1960 to cope with the Basildon New Town traffic. Photograph 1983.

above right
Rear view of the West Horndon house section. The platform canopy here has been removed. These stations are built in a dark red brick, in Flemish bond, with two courses of blue bricks at the head of the plinth, and three single course bands of blue brick across the windows on each floor. The two courses of corbelling in the gables are also in blue brick.

first right
Detail of window at West Horndon. All windows at these stations have yellow brick arches.

second right
At the 1880s new lines stations canopies were provided on the platform behind the main buildings. These canopies now survive only at Upminster and Laindon. None of the original valancing remains. The standard types of capital and bracket are seen in this view of Laindon.
The 'opposite' platform at these stations had only an open brick shelter. That at Ockendon remains and retains its valancing.

above

The main 1888 buildings at Pitsea are demolished but this station has the only remaining specimen of the standard footbridge design used on the 1880s new lines. (Few LT&SR footbridges remain, as most were replaced for electrification). The capitals are to the same design as on the platform canopies. These footbridges were originally covered.

below

The 1889 Southend (Central) down platform canopy. This has skylighting throughout. The roofing is carried on timber transverse and longitudinal beams.

The capitals are similar to those at the 1880s stations except for having three-branch decoration. The brackets are the same, although many columns at Southend have full-size brackets longitudinally as well as transversely.

below

Southend (Central) had a large porte-cochere on both the up and down sides, but only the down side one remains, as seen here in 1983. The 1889 station was built by Lucas & Aird, with ironwork supplied by A.Handyside & Co. of Derby.

bottom

Southend up side entrance as it has appeared since removal of the porte-cochere in 1972. The small replacement canopy is supported on original brackets. The lantern roof of the Booking Hall is seen behind.

above
  The Southend (Central) up platform canopy. This had two lines of columns when built in 1889, but was widened in the 1899 enlargements with a third line of columns (right) added, in the same style. The skylighting in this form, with arched supports, must date from 1899.

left and bottom left
  Westcliff was an additional station opened in 1895. The contract was given to Baker & Wiseman of Southend in June 1894, at £7,443. The overall arrangement is very similar to the 1885-92 stations (compare the West Horndon view), but the yellow brick construction and the flat-arched windows with red brick dressings create a rather different feel. The plinth is in engineering bricks. The corbelling is also in red brick, and there are two bands of red brick (plus a third across the first floor windows in the house section).

below
  The Westcliff canopies have these large 'LT&SR' roundel brackets, which were used 1894-1905 and can also be seen still at Plaistow, Upton Park, and East Ham.
  The down platform canopy at Westcliff is a 1980s reconstruction using original columns and brackets.

left

Thorpe Bay (1910) has a long frontage, with the Station Master's house at the east end, then the central hipped-roof Booking Hall section, then a lower section at the west end with two striped-gable pavilions. Again all is in yellow brick with red brick dressings. The windows have low segmental arches. This view shows the west end of the Booking Hall and one of the gabled pavilions.

middle

The up platform canopy at Thorpe Bay. The heavy Warren truss girders between the columns, supported on small brackets which are part of the main column casting, contrast with the plain RSJs used transversely.

The down platform canopy (right) is identically constructed. It was originally shorter and was extended to its present length in 1912. The small building behind it has two striped gables to the road.

bottom left

The canopy above the main entrance at Thorpe Bay, which remains in its original form, has these special brackets the design of which is derived from the platform canopy brackets.

bottom right

Detail of the platform canopy brackets at Thorpe Bay, which are to a unique design, albeit in the same basic three-roundel form as most LT&SR brackets.

top right
Benfleet in 1993. The *Southend Telegraph* noted at the time of the station's opening in December 1911 that 'there have been daily pilgrimages to the station and one and all have been loud in their praises'. The contractors were W.Pattinson & Sons of Ruskington.
Again construction is in yellow brick with red brick dressings.

top left and middle left
The Benfleet down platform canopy. Except for the different bracket design, the Benfleet canopies are the same as Thorpe Bay. This 'fishtail' valancing was used at Barking (1907, removed) and Dagenham Dock as well as Thorpe Bay and Benfleet.

middle right
This type of bracket was used at Benfleet and also at Plaistow in 1912. It is virtually as the LT&SR 1880s stations' brackets except for the form of the decoration in the large roundel. Interestingly the 1909/10 plans for Benfleet show these brackets as 'Messrs McFarlanes stock pattern', from which we may conclude that most LT&SR canopy brackets were 'ex catalogue' (except of course for the large 'LT&SR' type).

This photograph however is of the canopy at Frinton which was erected in the 1950s from second-hand components in place of the shorter 1888 canopy. It is an unsolved mystery as to which station these brackets could have come from!

right
The greatest engineering feature on the LT&SR lines in present-day Essex is the 14-arch Stifford Viaduct (south of Ockendon, GR 591801) completed in 1892. It was built for double track. The maximum height is only 32ft9in. The segmental arches have six rings.

CHAPTER EIGHT

THE COLNE VALLEY & HALSTEAD RAILWAY

Essex's third railway company, the Colne Valley & Halstead Railway, which remained independent until 1923, had some architecturally curious station buildings.

The initial section of the line from Chappel to Halstead, opened in 1860, was engineered by Nathaniel Beardmore who was better known as a water engineer and had been living at Broxbourne since 1855 in connection with his post as Engineer to the Lea Valley Navigation. However, the line's 'extension' from Halstead to Haverhill, opened 1861-3, had Joseph Cubitt as Consulting Engineer and Charles Brogden Sperling as sub-Engineer. Sperling, somewhat unusually, was from the local gentry, the heir to Dynes Hall, Great Maplestead. He had trained as an engineer in the 1840s and been with the Great Western and then the South Eastern.

The line's two surviving 1860s station buildings, White Colne and Sible Hedingham (the latter now carefully re-erected at the Colne Valley Railway preservation site), are to the same design even though White Colne is on the Beardmore section and Sible Hedingham on the Cubitt / Sperling section. As Beardmore definitely designed White Colne, one assumes the Board wanted the design replicated. These stations are built in a most unusual fashion mostly of white bricks face on, with quoins and dressings of red brick, plus some blue bricks in the window arches. The permanent (1862) building at Halstead, now demolished, was also built of white bricks face on, although to a completely different design; it was attributed to Cubitt.

above left and right
White Colne (originally 'Colne') station building (GR 871291) was at track level. Beardmore produced the plans for it in February 1860 and it was erected shortly after the line opened. The two windows either side of the drainpipes were originally doors, hence the interruptions in the two string courses of specially-shaped cream bricks. The 7ft-long plain red brick extension at the east end was probably done c1908 when the station reopened after a period of closure.

middle
This third view, from the southeast, shows the 'booking porch' provided on the east extension of the original building, plus the much larger separately-gabled brick extension on the south side, also done c1908.

bottom
One of the most remarkable railway survivals in Essex is the 1882 wooden station building from Earls Colne (originally Ford Gate) station, which became obsolete when the new buildings were provided in 1903/4. It was moved to H.W.Bone's builders yard at Colne Engaine (GR 851305), where it still resides. The windows and doors are replacements.

above

The 1903/4 buildings at Earls Colne (GR 848297) also remain, little altered, four decades after closure. (Since this photograph was taken in the 1970s, the house section of the building has been extended to the right, in the original style). The CV&HR received local financial support for this substantial Arts & Crafts-esque building.

J.E. Connor

middle

The railway is still readily traceable in Halstead. This is the crossing house in Parsonage Lane (GR 816302) which was erected by the LNER in 1930. J.W.Trudgett of Butt Road, Colchester, built it for £485.

bottom

Only one bridge survives intact on the Chappel – Halstead section of the CV&HR, at Station Road, Chappel (GR 897294). Still railway-maintained, it bears the number 'COV 1' under the latterday BR line reference system. This bridge would be Beardmore's work. The white brick segmental arch has five rings. There is heavy recent patching in bright red brick.

Chapter Nine

GOODS SHEDS, STABLES, SIGNAL BOXES AND OTHER ANCILLARY BUILDINGS

GOODS SHEDS

Around forty stations in Essex had sufficient goods traffic to justify a Goods Shed, but most of them have been demolished since the 1960s. The survivors, all readily accessible, are

Roydon	Brick	1840s	Derelict
Maldon East	Brick	1848	Brooks Bros, timber merchants (GR 852076)
Marks Tey	Timber	1850s?	Used as offices, much altered
Harwich	Brick	1865	Derelict
Rochford	Brick	1889	Community Centre / Hall
Maldon West	Brick	1889	Industrial Estate unit (GR 842061)
Chappel	Brick	1891	Railway Museum (photo p.38)
Wivenhoe	Brick	1903	Derelict

At some stations where goods traffic was more modest, a smaller 'Goods Lock-up' shed was provided on the platform. Examples survive at Hockley (p.34), Takeley, and Frinton.

Maldon West goods shed (1889), built to a standard design used on the new lines of 1888/9. An earlier example had however appeared at Mildenhall (1885).

The original 1860s timber goods shed at Wivenhoe burnt down in September 1900, and this brick replacement was provided in 1903, Kirk Knight & Co. getting the job in October 1902 at £1,709. There was another goods shed to this design at Rayne (1902, demolished).

STABLES

In the cities the railway companies maintained hundreds of horses for goods delivery, and in consequence had to build large stable blocks. In small towns however the railway stable would be for a few horses only (and indeed an outside contractor was often used instead). The three surviving railway stables in Essex are illustrated here (but see also Chappel, p.36 and p.39).

This charming three-horse stable at Manningtree was built c1900 in connection with the general reconstruction of the station.

Quite similar to Manningtree in style is the three-horse block built at Wivenhoe in 1903 at the same time as the new goods shed.

The six-horse stable provided at Harwich in 1913.

ENGINE SHEDS

Apart from a small fragment at Maldon East, the only surviving engine shed in Essex is the one-engine shed at Thaxted (1913).

WATER TANKS

Most water tanks were for locomotive purposes, but some also supplied water for stations. Examples can be seen at Chelmsford, Manningtree, and Thaxted. The railway companies were also compelled to build large reservoirs at some locations where supply was unreliable. The reservoir west of Southend Road, Rochford was built by the GER in 1904/5 to supply water to Southend.

In contrast the 1894 water tank at Manningtree is highly noticeable! The brick tower was built by Collins & Barber of Downham Market, and the cast-iron water tank was supplied by Head Wrightson for £114.

below The water tank built behind the east end of the down platform at Chelmsford in 1881 is so low as to be easily missed.

FOOTWARMER HOUSES

In the late nineteenth century, footwarmers were introduced on many lines to reduce the freezing of passengers. The metal footwarmers were filled with hot water in 'Footwarmer Houses' which were mostly located at those stations where trains began their journey. They survive at Ongar and Braintree. Footwarmers became redundant when the general steam heating of carriages was introduced.

The 1899 Braintree Footwarmer House.

SIGNAL BOXES

The only traditional type signal boxes still in use on the national rail system in Essex are Ingatestone, East Gate Junction (Colchester), Thorpe-le-Soken, Clacton, and Frinton. However another twenty signal boxes remain in situ, either in other uses on the national network or at preservation sites.

above
  GER boxes were built with hipped roofs until 1876. This 1981 view shows the 1875-built GER Type 1 box at Wrabness. This has since been moved to the Colne Valley Railway where it is in use at the east end of their line as 'Nunnery Junction' (only visible from trains).

below
  Mistley box (see also photo p.16) was built in 1882 as part of the improvements carried out on the Harwich branch prior to the opening of Parkeston Quay. The GER at this time was entering a period of very decorative signal box designs. Mistley is to the GER Type 3 design, featuring seven-pane windows, 'rusticated' boarding, and a splendid bargeboard design. The iron brackets supporting the landing are to the same pattern as those on contemporary platform canopies (see Dovercourt photo p.42).
  After being abolished in the 1985 Harwich branch resignalling, Mistley box was moved to the East Anglian Railway Museum, and reopened as 'Chappel North' in 1986. The 27-lever McKenzie & Holland 1873 Patent 5in pitch lever frame is the original 1882 frame. The box can be visited on operating days.

above
After 1886 most GER boxes were built to the much plainer GER Type 7 design, the standard version of which is illustrated by Chappel box at p.39. Chelmsford box, illustrated here, was a Type 7 box with an unusually steeply-pitched roof. It was built in 1899, as part of the general improvements to the station effected then, on a very tall brick base alongside the viaduct. It was abolished in 1996 but is still in situ.

In the years around 1960, many lines in Essex were resignalled in connection with electrification, with new modern power signal boxes controlling much longer sections of line than had been possible with the former mechanical/semaphore signalling. This is Pitsea box, opened in 1960, to a standard Eastern Region design with large sun baffle to keep direct sunlight off the control panels. However, all these boxes have themselves now been abolished under further resignallings. Other abolished boxes of this type still in use as offices etc are Southend Central, Witham, and Harlow Mill.

Frinton gate hut appears to go back to the 1880s, but somewhat in the 'family broom' tradition! – in particular it had to be repaired after bomb damage in 1943. Since 1974 its only function has been to work the signals protecting the level crossing. These are now the only remaining semaphore signals on the national network in Essex, save for some in the sidings at Clacton.

Traditional manned level crossing gates survive at Chitts Hill (west of Colchester), Alresford Station, Alresford Coach Road, Thorrington, Great Bentley, Burrs Road (Clacton), Frinton, and Elsenham. Chitts Hill, illustrated here, has a curved-roof brick gateman's hut of the type erected by the GER around 1900.

All these crossings have concrete gate posts, which became common in East Anglia from the 1920s in lieu of the wooden posts used previously.

CHAPTER TEN

POST-1920 STATION BUILDINGS

The Great Eastern Railway was absorbed into the new **London & North Eastern Railway** in 1923, but it was some years before that company provided any new station building in Essex. The first was Clacton where the new station of 1929, a typical piece of neo-Georgian of the period, replaced the original timber buildings of 1882.

A much bigger job was the widening of the main line from Romford to Shenfield, carried out in 1930-33. This involved the total reconstruction of Romford station and the replacement of most of the existing buildings at Harold Wood, Brentwood, and Shenfield. The new buildings were all in a plain neo-Georgian verging on 1930s modern. The new platform canopies were still of traditional design.

The first LNER building in Essex to fully embrace the 'modern style' was the new Loughton station of 1940. This was designed by the architect John Murray Easton who was commissioned in 1937 to prepare plans for the rebuilding of all stations north of Woodford. Loughton was a showpiece but nothing was even produced on paper for the other stations, in the event.

The ex - London Tilbury & Southend lines passed into the **London Midland & Scottish Railway** in 1923. The LMS was forced to carry out major improvements on the LT&S to cope with the burgeoning outer suburban and Southend commuter traffics. The Barking-Upminster section was quadrupled in 1931/2 and all the stations rebuilt in a modern brick style. This was followed by new stations at Southend East (1932), Chalkwell (1933), and Leigh-on-Sea (1933). Of these three only Chalkwell remains intact.

The other major project of the LMS period was the reconstruction of Tilbury Riverside in 1926-30, a joint project with the Port of London Authority, with Sir Edwin Cooper as architect. The *magnum opus* was the Baggage Hall, now the London International Cruise Terminal, the adjacent station concourse being more workaday. The Floating Landing Stage was provided for ocean liners and the Gravesend ferry.

After nationalisation in 1948, the whole Essex railway system fell into the **British Railways Eastern Region**. A number of station rebuilding projects took place under the 1950s 'Modernisation Plan', of which Harlow Town (1960) is regarded as one of the finest stations of that era. Elsewhere on the ex-GER lines there were new Booking Halls at Bishops Stortford (1960) and Colchester (1961). More was done on the ex-LT&SR lines, with new station buildings in Essex at Grays (c1955), Purfleet (c1960) and Stanford-le-Hope (c1960).

Several further new station buildings have followed since the 1970s, but it is not yet the time for the historian to pass judgment on them.

above left
The central portion of the 1929 Clacton station (there are also single-storey angled wings either side), which is built in dark red brick with stone dressings. There was until recently a small balcony above the entrance.

left
The main (down side) entrance block at Brentwood, photographed when new in 1934. This is actually a two-storey structure. A second Booking Office building was provided on the up side in 1933, but no longer exists. Note the diaperwork in the gable, a feature of all these stations.
New platform buildings and canopies were provided at Brentwood in 1933 on the new up side platform (demolished except for a short section of canopy) and the central island platform (still in situ), but the 1884 canopy on the down side platform merely received new valancing to match the others.

above right
A 1934 view of Shenfield, showing the new buildings and canopies on platforms 3/4 and 5. These remain in full. A new road frontage building was provided in 1933 but has since been replaced by an office block.

top left

A platform view of the 1940 Loughton station, which comprises two island platforms on embankment and a road level Booking Hall with a false barrel vault ceiling. All the brickwork is of 'golden brown' bricks laid in an unusual bond of two stretchers and one header in every course, with the horizontal joints accentuated. The signal box and electric substation are similarly constructed. The concrete platform canopies have like most of their kind needed modification subsequently.

top right

Detail of the 1933 up platform buildings at Leigh-on-Sea (which have unfortunately been rewindowed since this 1990s photograph). All the new LMS stations on the LT&S were in red brick, in English bond, with the horizontal joints heavily accentuated, and with these special thin bricks for the door and window surrounds. The stations between Barking and Upminster, and Southend East, had small-pane windows, but Chalkwell and Leigh-on-Sea a year later had these more modern windows with horizontal glazing bars only.

All these stations had steel canopies of simple lines (concrete canopies were not introduced by the LMS until later in the 1930s).

middle

A recent view of the grand Tilbury Riverside Baggage Hall, which has recently found use as a concert venue as well as still serving for the Cruise Terminal.
Port of Tilbury London Ltd

bottom

The Tilbury Riverside station concourse. This still exists, as the whole station is listed, but is now boarded off from public access. Although there is no contemporary reference, the roof appears to be second-hand from the previous (1906) concourse building.

GENEALOGY OF ESSEX RAILWAY COMPANIES
with line opening dates and absorption dates

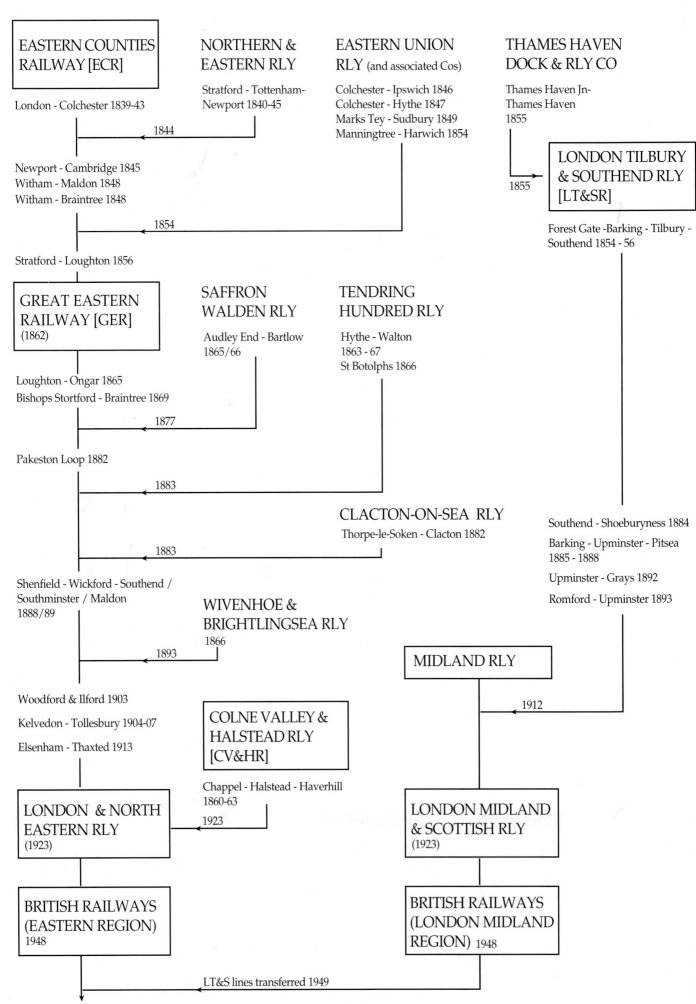

EASTERN COUNTIES RAILWAY [ECR]

London - Colchester 1839-43

NORTHERN & EASTERN RLY

Stratford - Tottenham-Newport 1840-45

EASTERN UNION RLY (and associated Cos)

Colchester - Ipswich 1846
Colchester - Hythe 1847
Marks Tey - Sudbury 1849
Manningtree - Harwich 1854

THAMES HAVEN DOCK & RLY CO

Thames Haven Jn-Thames Haven 1855

1844

Newport - Cambridge 1845
Witham - Maldon 1848
Witham - Braintree 1848

LONDON TILBURY & SOUTHEND RLY [LT&SR]

1855

Forest Gate -Barking - Tilbury - Southend 1854 - 56

1854

Stratford - Loughton 1856

GREAT EASTERN RAILWAY [GER] (1862)

SAFFRON WALDEN RLY

Audley End - Bartlow 1865/66

TENDRING HUNDRED RLY

Hythe - Walton 1863 - 67
St Botolphs 1866

Loughton - Ongar 1865
Bishops Stortford - Braintree 1869

1877

Pakeston Loop 1882

1883

CLACTON-ON-SEA RLY

Thorpe-le-Soken - Clacton 1882

Southend - Shoeburyness 1884

Barking - Upminster - Pitsea 1885 - 1888

Upminster - Grays 1892

Romford - Upminster 1893

1883

Shenfield - Wickford - Southend / Southminster / Maldon 1888/89

WIVENHOE & BRIGHTLINGSEA RLY
1866

1893

MIDLAND RLY

Woodford & Ilford 1903

Kelvedon - Tollesbury 1904-07

Elsenham - Thaxted 1913

COLNE VALLEY & HALSTEAD RLY [CV&HR]

Chappel - Halstead - Haverhill 1860-63

1923

1912

LONDON & NORTH EASTERN RLY (1923)

LONDON MIDLAND & SCOTTISH RLY (1923)

BRITISH RAILWAYS (EASTERN REGION) 1948

BRITISH RAILWAYS (LONDON MIDLAND REGION) 1948

LT&S lines transferred 1949